To

From

Date

Reawaken Your Spirit, Rediscover Your God-Given Gifts, and Reclaim Your Joy

Rising from the Rut

ISIS BRADFORD

DaySpring
LIVE YOUR FAITH

Rising from the Rut: Reawaken Your Spirit, Rediscover Your God-Given Gifts, and Reclaim Your Joy

First Edition, October 2025

Published by:

DaySpring

21154 Highway 16 East
Siloam Springs, AR 72761
dayspring.com

Written by: Isis Bradford
Cover Design by: Jenna Wilusz

Printed in Vietnam
Prime: U4520
ISBN: 979-8-88603-380-9

Contents

Letter from the Author

There's a certain kind of agony that doesn't scream—it whispers and follows you in all that you do. It's the ache of feeling stuck and the subtle but unyielding doubt that maybe you've lost your way. That heaviness that creeps into your mornings, the lingering thought that there's got to be more than this. I've felt it too.

Several years ago, I found myself in the deepest rut of my life. I was financially strapped, selling plasma twice a week at a blood bank just to make ends meet. My faith was still there, but it felt distant, like a faint echo in the chaos of my circumstances. I knew God had called me to entrepreneurship—I could constantly feel the tug of that vision in my heart—but at the time, I had no idea why or how it would happen. Every step forward felt like trudging through mud, and I doubted my strength to keep going.

It was in that season of uncertainty that I started exploring simple, practical ways to reconnect with myself, God, and the vision He had placed in me. I didn't know it then, but the activities and reflections in this book were birthed from that season. They weren't just ideas; they were lifelines. Step by step, God met me in the mess, and I began to see a way out of the rut.

Later, when I started my career as a marketing strategist and business coach, I thought success would mean equipping others with the perfect strategies to grow their businesses. But I quickly realized there's no amount of strategy that can overcome a soul stuck in survival mode. Whether it was clients who were spinning their wheels or my own moments of burnout, one thing became clear: When you feel disconnected from or unsure of your purpose, no amount of external effort will fill the gap. That's when I decided to merge my gifts and my story into a devotional that doesn't just inspire action—it inspires *transformation*.

The truth is, the journey out of a rut doesn't require a grand, dramatic overhaul. It's the tiny, consistent steps that reconnect your vision. It's rediscovering the gifts He's placed within you and reclaiming the joy that's been buried beneath the weight of discouragement.

Take, for example, the story of Zora Neale Hurston, world-renowned writer and anthropologist and one of my personal inspirations. Although she was born in poverty and grew up in the segregated South during a time when opportunities for Black women were severely limited, Hurston didn't let the constraints of her circumstances define her. She traveled across the South and the Caribbean, collecting stories, folklore, and wisdom that shaped her writing and cemented her legacy. Her courage to step out of the familiar and embrace new perspectives taught me the power of changing your inputs. Sometimes the key to reigniting your spirit is as simple as exposing yourself to something fresh—whether it's a new environment, a new habit, or a new way of thinking.

That same spirit of exploration is at the heart of this book. Each devotion offers a practice to help you reawaken your soul, rediscover your God-given gifts, and reclaim your joy. These aren't lofty ideas—they're grounded, actionable steps that helped me when I felt like I had nothing left to give. Whether it's starting a Breakthrough Journal to document moments of clarity or creating "Theme Days" to bring intentionality to your week, these practices are designed to help you take practical steps toward the abundant life God has for you.

So, dear reader, I want you to know something: Your rut is not your destiny. The feelings of stagnancy, the weariness, the questioning—they're temporary. God didn't create you to live a life weighed down by uncertainty and routine. He created you with a purpose, and no matter how buried it feels right now, that purpose is still alive within you.

As you journey through this book, my prayer is that you'll feel seen, understood, and empowered. I hope you'll laugh, cry, and maybe even wrestle with some of the truths God reveals to you. Most of all, I hope you'll rediscover what it means to be fully alive—to wake up each day knowing you are walking in step with the Creator who designed you for greatness.

The rut you're in doesn't define you. What defines you is the God who holds your future, who gives you the strength to rise, and who is waiting to meet you in the small, steady steps of faith. Together, let's take those steps. Let's rediscover the gifts within us. Let's reclaim the joy that's rightfully ours. And let's rise.

With love and purpose,

Write Your Legacy

Your life is a gift from God,
and what you do with it is your gift to Him.

— UNKNOWN

In 1888, at the young age of fifty-six, Ludvig Nobel died of a heart attack. Soon after, his brother, Alfred, picked up a newspaper, turned to the obituary, and froze. The shock of such a loss would make anyone stop in their tracks, but there was another reason his feet were glued to the ground. There, staring back at Alfred, was his own obituary. The newspapers had confused him with his deceased brother, who shared an uncanny resemblance. What surprised Nobel the most wasn't his brother's passing or the obituary mistake; it was how the world saw him: "The merchant of death is dead," the headline declared.

Alfred Nobel was famous for creating dynamite. Today we know dynamite for its dangerous explosions and loud attacks, but Nobel created it to improve the world. He hoped that dynamite would make the use of nitroglycerin safer for construction projects like tunnel digging, rock blasting, and railroad laying. Instead, his invention was exploited as a weapon of war.

That morning, while reading his erroneous obituary, he faced a gut-wrenching question: *Is this how I want to be remembered?* He decided it was not. He chose to rewrite his story, and thus came the Nobel Prize. Born from this moment of reckoning, these awards now celebrate those who push humanity forward through science, literature, and peace. In just one bold decision, Alfred Nobel transformed his legacy from one of destruction to one of progress.

Picture the headline that might one day carry your name. Would it speak of kindness shown to strangers? Of quiet moments spent nurturing family bonds? Of creative courage and brave pivots? Your legacy isn't some mysterious thing in a faraway land–it's alive in the way you treat others, the work you do, the values you stand for, the mercy you showed when judgment was easier, and the truth you spoke when silence was safer. The hope you planted in soil others deemed barren. Whether we realize it or not, we're all writing our legacies right now. Every choice, every action, adds another line to our story.

Psalm 90:12 says it clearly: "Teach us to number our days, that we may gain a heart of wisdom." Life is precious, each moment an opportunity to shape something lasting. In the sweep of time, our lives may seem brief, but their impact can ripple through generations, touching souls in ways only God can fully understand.

In the end, a meaningful legacy isn't measured in monuments or accolades but in the lives transformed through your journey. Through faith, purpose, and wise counsel we can craft legacies that endure beyond our years. So, what will your story be?

Teach us to number our days, that we may gain a heart of wisdom.

— PSALM 90:12

LORD,

help me to see my life through Your eyes.
Teach me to number my days and recognize
the opportunities You've given me to leave
a legacy of love, kindness, and faith.
May every choice and action I take reflect
Your purpose and bring glory to Your name.

AMEN.

QUESTIONS TO CONSIDER:

1. What do you want to be remembered for when your story is told?
2. Are your current actions aligning with the legacy you hope to leave behind?
3. What values or principles are most important for you to pass on to others?
4. How do you reflect God's love and wisdom in your daily life?
5. Who in your life is impacted most by your words and actions?

RIGHT NOW:

- Write down three core values that define how you want to live your life.
- Identify one recent action or decision that reflected these values and one that didn't.

THIS WEEK:

- Write your own obituary, focusing on the legacy you want to leave behind. Be honest about what you want your life to look like when all is said and done.
- Share your "legacy vision" with someone you trust and ask for their perspective.

MOVING FORWARD:

- Reflect on your daily habits and routines. Are they moving you closer to the legacy you want to create? Start making small adjustments to align your actions with your vision.
- Begin a gratitude practice where you write down one way you positively impacted someone each day. Over time, this will help you track the legacy you are actively building.

Reminder:

Every choice you make writes a line in your story. Choose actions that leave a legacy of love, faith, and purpose.

Change Your Inputs

If you change the way you look at things,

the things you look at change.

— WAYNE DYER

What are you allowing to shape your thoughts? The stories we hear, the environments we inhabit, and the voices we engage with all influence the way we see the world and the work we do within it.

In 1937 anthropologist Zora Neale Hurston published her now-classic novel, *Their Eyes Were Watching God.* At the time, Hurston was immersed in the cultural vibrancy of the Harlem Renaissance, but she didn't limit her influences to her immediate surroundings. She traveled extensively across the Caribbean and the American South, collecting stories, folklore, and music that infused her writing with authenticity and depth. By stepping outside of her comfort zone and engaging with diverse perspectives, Zora found the creative spark that helped shape her voice and legacy.

Her willingness to broaden her inputs brought fresh energy to her work, allowing her to craft narratives that remain timeless. Zora's story reminds us that transformation often comes when we expose ourselves to new ideas, environments, and voices; and that stagnation steps in when we recycle the same influences without venturing into the unfamiliar.

Romans 12:2 urges us to "be transformed by the renewing of your mind." Renewal requires intentionality. What are you consuming daily?

Are your inputs inspiring you to grow closer to God's purpose for your life? Are they expanding your vision or keeping you in a cycle of sameness?

Much like Zora's travels enriched her creativity, we are called to explore and invite new influences that align with God's truth. This doesn't mean abandoning the familiar but rather complementing it with voices that challenge and inspire you. It might look like reading a book on a topic you've never studied, listening to a podcast outside your usual genre, or engaging in meaningful conversations with people who see the world differently.

Zora's travels were not just physical—they were spiritual and intellectual journeys as well. She believed that the richness of life came from embracing diverse stories and perspectives, and her work reflected that belief. Sometimes we need to step out of the echo chambers of our own making and seek new voices through books, music, sermons, or even moments in nature.

Each new input becomes an opportunity for God to speak to you in fresh and unexpected ways. If Zora Neale Hurston had stayed within the confines of Harlem, she might have missed the folktales and cultural treasures that made her work iconic. Just like you might be missing the creative, spiritual, emotional, and intellectual treasures God is waiting to reveal to you.

Growth starts when we dare to change the way we look at things. Just as Zora Neale Hurston found her unique, creative voice through diverse influences, you, too, can discover new dimensions of your faith, purpose, and calling when you step beyond the usual and embrace the new.

Be transformed by the renewing of your mind.

—ROMANS 12:2

HEAVENLY FATHER,

open my heart and mind to new influences that align with Your truth. Help me discern what to let in and what to let go, so I can grow closer to Your purpose for my life. Expand my vision, renew my thoughts, and guide me toward what inspires and uplifts me.

AMEN.

QUESTIONS TO CONSIDER:

1. What influences are currently shaping my thoughts and beliefs?
2. Are there any inputs that are causing me to feel stagnant or uninspired?
3. How can I invite more God-centered influences into my daily life?
4. When was the last time I intentionally stepped out of my comfort zone?
5. What specific areas of my life could benefit from fresh perspectives?

RIGHT NOW:

- Write down three sources of input that you engage with daily (e.g., books, social media, conversations). Reflect on whether they align with your faith and inspire growth.
- Identify one new input to explore today, such as listening to a sermon or podcast or reading a book from a genre or perspective you've never considered.

THIS WEEK:

- Spend at least thirty minutes engaging with something new: Visit a local museum, take a walk in a new neighborhood, or watch a documentary about a topic you know little about.
- Replace one negative or stagnant influence (like a toxic social media account or unhelpful routine) with something that uplifts your spirit or broadens your perspective.

MOVING FORWARD:

- Make it a habit to intentionally seek out one new source of inspiration each month, whether it's a new author, a different worship playlist, or a thought-provoking conversation.
- Commit to regularly evaluating your inputs, ensuring they align with your faith and encourage growth in all areas of your life.

Reminder:
Expanding your inputs opens the door for God to reveal treasures that inspire, challenge, and transform you.

Chart Your Course

A journey of a thousand miles begins with a single step.

— LAO TZU

The act of stepping into the unfamiliar has a way of reshaping the ordinary. Jessica Nabongo, the first Black woman to travel to every country in the world, didn't begin her journey with the intention of making history. It started simply, with curiosity—a decision to say yes to new experiences. Whether wandering through bustling markets in Morocco, hiking verdant trails in Central America, or savoring quiet moments in a European café, Jessica's travels were not just about crossing borders but about finding beauty in the small, deliberate adventures that defined her routine.

While her story is extraordinary, the principle she lived by—openness to discovery—is something we all can embrace. It doesn't require a plane ticket or a passport. We don't need to traverse continents to spark inspiration or break free from the monotony of daily life. A simple micro-adventure—like exploring a local park, trying a new dance class, or finding a new coffee spot—can transform our perspective. Jessica reminds us that it's not the distance traveled but the mindset of curiosity and intentionality that breathes life into these moments.

Isaiah 43:19 captures this spirit of renewal: "See, I am doing a new thing! Now it springs up; do you not perceive it? I am making a way in the wilderness and streams in the wasteland." God often works in the ordinary, inviting us to step out of the routine and experience His creation in fresh ways. Micro-adventures become pathways to recognize His presence, reminding us of the beauty and creativity He has placed around us.

Julia Cameron, author of *The Artist's Way*, advocates for "artist dates"—intentional solo outings designed to reignite creativity. A visit to a botanical garden, a walk at sunrise, or browsing a quaint antique store can do more than spark inspiration; they can reconnect us to joy. Cameron's practice mirrors the essence of micro-adventures, showing how small, deliberate actions can stir the heart and awaken the soul.

Even science affirms this truth. Studies reveal that breaking from routine and trying new experiences not only boosts mental health but also sparks creativity and reduces stress. The unfamiliar stretches us, forming new neural connections and opening our minds to possibilities we may have overlooked. In those moments, we become more attuned to God's gentle guidance, discovering His purpose for us in the most unexpected places.

What would it look like to bring this sense of adventure into your own life? Like Jessica Nabongo's travels or Julia Cameron's artist dates, these small, intentional acts invite joy and transformation. They become a way to embrace the richness of life and rediscover the God who is always doing something new.

**See, I am doing a new thing!
Now it springs up;
do you not perceive it?
I am making a way in the wilderness
and streams in the wasteland.**

— ISAIAH 43:19

LORD,
thank You for the beauty and creativity You've placed in the world around me. Help me to see Your presence in the ordinary, and give me the courage to step into the new things You are calling me to. Open my heart to the small adventures that reveal Your joy and purpose.
AMEN.

QUESTIONS TO CONSIDER:

1. What routines or habits in my life feel stagnant or uninspired?
2. When was the last time I intentionally sought out something new or unfamiliar?
3. How can I incorporate small moments of joy and discovery into my daily life?
4. What has God placed around me that I may be overlooking?
5. How can stepping outside of my routine bring me closer to God's presence and purpose?

RIGHT NOW:

- Identify one small micro-adventure you can take today, such as visiting a new coffee shop, exploring a different walking route, or reading a book from a genre you don't typically choose.
- Spend five minutes journaling about how stepping out of your comfort zone makes you feel—both the excitement and the hesitation.

THIS WEEK:

- Choose one intentional outing to spark creativity or joy, like visiting a nearby town, going to a farmer's market, or a scenic spot near your home. Take note of what you observe and how it makes you feel.
- Try something you've been putting off because it feels too small or insignificant, such as starting a creative project or exploring a new part of your neighborhood.

MOVING FORWARD:

- Make it a habit to schedule micro-adventures into your routine—whether weekly or monthly—to intentionally invite new experiences into your life.
- Reflect regularly on how these small acts of exploration are shaping your mindset and drawing you closer to God.

Reminder:

Small, deliberate steps into the unfamiliar can transform your perspective and awaken your soul to God's newness.

Break a Rule

Rules are not necessarily sacred, principles are.

— FRANKLIN D. ROOSEVELT

There are moments in life when the rules we were taught to follow begin to feel like a cage. Tara Westover knows this intimately. Her memoir, *Educated*, chronicles a childhood shaped by rigid, unyielding rules. Raised in a survivalist family in rural Idaho, she lived without formal schooling, avoided modern medicine, and learned that questioning her parents' authority was unthinkable. These unwritten rules sought to define her identity and dictate her potential. Yet Tara sensed that something greater was calling her beyond the boundaries that confined her.

Her decision to break free and pursue education was not an act of rebellion but a journey of faith and determination. With no formal schooling, she began teaching herself math, science, and grammar, equipping herself to take the ACT. That step of courage earned her a place at Brigham Young University, setting her on a path that would lead to Cambridge and Harvard. Tara's story is less about breaking rules and more about discerning which boundaries hold us back from the life God has designed for us.

Mark 2:27 tells us, "The Sabbath was made for man, not man for the Sabbath." This verse is a powerful reminder that rules are meant to serve, not enslave. While structure and guidelines can provide safety and order, they can also become chains when they no longer align with God's higher purpose. Tara's journey reveals the importance of evaluating the rules we've internalized—whether from family, culture, or our own fears—and asking if they reflect God's truth or simply human limitations.

Breaking free from limiting rules requires courage and discernment. For Tara, stepping into the unknown came with significant challenges. She faced strained family relationships, moments of inconceivable isolation, and the discomfort of redefining who she was. Yet through it all, she found freedom, purpose, and the ability to use her story to inspire others. Her life illustrates that sometimes growth requires us to confront the rules that confine us and embrace the principles that liberate us.

What unspoken rules are shaping your life today? Perhaps it's the belief that you're not capable of pursuing a new dream or that failure will define you. Maybe it's the idea that success must fit a specific mold. These rules, often deeply ingrained, can keep us from fully stepping into God's plan. Tara's journey reminds us that we have the power to question these limitations and align our lives with God's truth.

Her story is a testament to the courage it takes to break free from the confines of human-made rules and step into the abundant life God offers. By evaluating the beliefs and boundaries that shape your decisions, you can discern which to release and which to embrace. When you do, you'll find that God's principles lead to freedom, transformation, and a life lived fully in His purpose. The question is: What rules should you break today?

The Sabbath was made for man, not man for the Sabbath.

— MARK 2:27

LORD,
thank You for the courage to evaluate the rules and beliefs that shape my life. Help me discern what aligns with Your truth, and give me the boldness to break free from anything that holds me back from living fully in Your purpose. Guide my steps as I seek to embrace Your principles over human limitations.
AMEN.

QUESTIONS TO CONSIDER:

1. Are there rules or beliefs you follow that no longer align with God's calling for your life?
2. How can you discern the difference between God's principles and human-made limitations?
3. What fears or challenges might be keeping you from stepping into something new?
4. Have you experienced a time when breaking free from a limiting belief brought you closer to God's purpose?
5. How can you seek God's guidance as you evaluate the boundaries in your life?

RIGHT NOW:

- Identify one limiting belief or "rule" you've internalized. Write it down and pray over it, asking God to reveal whether it aligns with His truth.
- Reflect on an area in your life where you feel restricted or stuck. Consider if this is due to a self-imposed rule or external expectation.

THIS WEEK:

- Take one small, courageous step to challenge a limiting rule in your life. This could mean starting a project you've put off, having a difficult conversation, or exploring a dream you've dismissed.
- Journal about how this process feels and what you're learning about yourself and God's guidance.

MOVING FORWARD:

- Regularly evaluate the "rules" you live by. Ask yourself: *Are they serving God's purpose for my life or holding me back?*
- Surround yourself with people who encourage and challenge you to live boldly in alignment with God's truth.

Reminder:

Freedom begins when we replace limiting rules with God's principles, stepping into the abundant life He has designed for us.

Chase Your Curiosities

Find something you're passionate about and keep tremendously interested in it.

— JULIA CHILD

Julia Child didn't grow up dreaming of being a chef. She didn't spend her college years perfecting recipes or shadowing cooks. In fact, Julia didn't even know how to boil an egg until her mid-thirties. Her story took an unexpected turn when her husband's job called them to France. It was there, while simply playing around with flavors and experimenting in her kitchen, that her curiosity for food blossomed into a passion that eventually redefined American cuisine.

This passion led her to a single cooking class at Le Cordon Bleu. Julia didn't take that class to become famous or build a career. She took it because she wanted to learn, to play, to have fun in the kitchen. There was no pressure, no rush to monetize her new interest or turn it into something grand. She simply allowed herself the freedom to play, make mistakes, try again, and let her curiosity lead the way. That spirit of exploration and play laid the foundation for her legacy as one of the most beloved culinary figures of the twentieth century.

Your curiosity can unlock doors you didn't even know existed and lead you to new understandings. Proverbs 1:5 (ESV) says, "Let the wise hear and increase in learning, and the one who understands obtain guidance." Understanding includes not only gaining knowledge but also recognizing God's promises and desires for our lives. God calls us to use the gifts He's given us, and He promises to work all things together for good. Chasing your curiosities, then, becomes an act of faith—a way to show God that you trust His promises and believe He has a plan for your gifts and passions. Whether Julia intellectualized that or not, it's exactly what she was doing. By following her curiosity, she stepped into something greater than she could have ever imagined, allowing God to weave her playful exploration into a legacy that inspired generations.

Studies in neuroscience reveal that learning through exploration and creativity stimulates the brain, builds new neural pathways, and increases mental agility. But play isn't just good for your brain—it's good for your soul. When you try something new without pressure, you create space for God to reveal His creativity and purpose in unexpected ways.

Julia once said, "No one is born a great cook; one learns by doing." Her words remind us that greatness is rarely found in natural talent but in the willingness to engage fully with life. Play isn't wasted time—it's the fertile ground where passions grow. When you give yourself permission to experiment and enjoy the process, you might uncover gifts, skills, and callings you never expected.

So, what's something you've always wanted to try but never allowed yourself to? It doesn't have to be productive or practical—just playful. Whether it's painting, baking, dancing, or learning a new language, let yourself have fun with it. As Julia's story teaches us, the act of playing is where adventures begin.

Let the wise hear and increase in learning, and the one who understands obtain guidance.

— PROVERBS 1:5 ESV

HEAVENLY FATHER,

thank You for the gifts of curiosity and the joy that come from exploring Your world. Help me embrace the freedom to play, learn, and grow without fear of failure or the need for perfection. May my heart remain open to discovering the passions and gifts You've placed within me.

AMEN.

QUESTIONS TO CONSIDER:

1. When was the last time you allowed yourself to try something new without worrying about the outcome?
2. What are some interests or hobbies you've been curious about but hesitant to explore?
3. How does the idea of "play" fit into your current understanding of learning and growth?
4. Are there ways you've put pressure on yourself to turn a passion into a result, rather than enjoying the process?
5. How might exploring your curiosities reveal new aspects of God's creativity and purpose for your life?

RIGHT NOW:

- Make a list of three things you've always wanted to try but have put off. Choose one to explore this week, approaching it with a playful, pressure-free mindset.
- Set aside thirty minutes today to experiment with something new—whether it's trying a recipe, doodling, or learning a few words in a new language.

THIS WEEK:

- Plan a "play session" where you intentionally spend time exploring one of your curiosities. Let go of expectations and simply enjoy the process.
- Reflect on what you felt during this time of exploration. Did it bring you joy, inspiration, or a new perspective?

MOVING FORWARD:

- Make space in your schedule for regular "play" moments—times when you engage in something just for the joy of it.
- Pay attention to how these playful moments enhance your creativity, connection with God, and overall sense of wonder.

Reminder:

Play is not wasted time—it's where joy meets discovery and passion begins to grow.

Work Backward

Begin with the end in mind.

— STEPHEN COVEY

Catherine Johnson, the legendary NASA "computer" and mathematician, is best known for her critical role in some of the most iconic space missions in history. As depicted in the book and film *Hidden Figures*, Johnson's groundbreaking calculations helped send astronauts into orbit and bring them safely home. One of her most famous achievements was reverse-engineering the mission plan for John Glenn's orbit around Earth. Starting with the desired landing point, she meticulously worked backward through three orbits, all the way to the launch pad.

Johnson's ability to visualize the end result and map the necessary steps backward was nothing short of extraordinary. By breaking down the mission into manageable stages, she turned an overwhelming challenge into something achievable—and thus helped Glenn become the first American to orbit earth.

Proverbs 16:3 says, "Commit to the Lord whatever you do, and he will establish your plans." Catherine's method of reverse engineering reflects this wisdom. When we begin with the end in mind and commit our plans to God, we invite Him to guide our steps and establish a clear path forward. Whether your goal is as ambitious as launching a rocket or as personal as building a healthier lifestyle, starting with the desired outcome can provide clarity and direction.

Think about the goals God has placed on your heart. Do you have a dream you've been putting off because it feels too big, or a calling that seems impossible to achieve? Work backward. For example, if you dream of writing a book, start by imagining the finished product in a reader's hands. How will the book end? How should the reader feel once they've finished? What will they take away from your book? From there, incorporate your goals into the outline, drafting, and writing process.

Catherine Johnson's work also reminds us of the importance of faith in the process. She didn't have the luxury of error—astronauts' lives depended on her calculations. Yet she approached her work with confidence, precision, and trust in her ability to solve complex problems. Similarly, when we commit our plans to God, we can trust that He will equip us with the wisdom and resources we need to succeed.

Reverse-engineering isn't just a practical strategy; it's a spiritual discipline. It requires us to envision the future God has for us and trust Him with the details. By working backward, we acknowledge that God knows the end from the beginning and invite Him to guide us through each step of the journey.

So, what's your end goal? Whether it's starting a business, deepening your relationships, or growing in your faith, take a cue from Catherine Johnson. Start with the end in mind, commit your plans to God, and trust that He will establish your steps. With faith, focus, and intentional action, even the loftiest goals become possible.

Commit to the LORD whatever you do, and He will establish your plans.

— PROVERBS 16:3

LORD,

thank You for being the ultimate planner and for seeing the end from the beginning. Help me to trust in Your guidance as I set goals and break them down into steps. Give me the faith and perseverance to follow through, knowing You are with me every step of the way.

AMEN.

QUESTIONS TO CONSIDER:

1. What is a goal God has placed on your heart that feels overwhelming or out of reach?
2. Have you taken the time to imagine the end result of this goal? What does it look like?
3. What steps might you need to take to work backward from your desired outcome?
4. How can committing your plans to God change the way you approach your goals?
5. What does it look like to trust God with both the details and the outcome of your journey?

RIGHT NOW:

- Write down one big goal or dream you've been putting off because it feels too overwhelming.
- Spend ten minutes visualizing the end result and what it would feel like to achieve it.

THIS WEEK:

- Break down your goal into smaller, actionable steps. Identify at least three steps you can take this week to move closer to that vision.
- Reflect on one resource or support system (a person, a book, or a skill) you might need to help you along the way.

MOVING FORWARD:

- Commit your plans to God in prayer daily. Ask for His wisdom and guidance as you take steps toward your goal.
- Revisit your goal regularly and refine the steps as needed, trusting that God will direct your path.

Reminder:
The biggest dreams are accomplished one small step at a time. Start with the end in mind, and trust God with the journey.

"Write the vision,
no matter
how big it is."

INTERVIEW 1:

Joy After Depression

BY: NAFEESAH LEVERETT
CREDIT ANALYST | ENTREPRENEUR

1: What are you reigniting, reawakening, rediscovering, or reclaiming in this season?

A: I'm rediscovering joy and confidence after depression, and I'm reigniting my faith in Christ. This journey began in 2016 after being in and out of abusive relationships, carrying mountains of shame, and struggling to find myself. I was exhausted and desperate, and needed a change.

2: What challenges have you faced in this process, and what have they taught you?

A: I didn't know what I looked like outside of depression. I was used to the chaos and didn't know that life could get any better. I had to look myself in the mirror, accept the responsibility that I played in this journey, and ask God for courage to not go back to my past.
I did a lot of journaling, praying, sharing my testimony, and hearing the testimony of others. It helped me realize that I was not alone and that there is hope on the other side of my pain. God is patient, kind, understanding, and loving. When I came back to Him, he welcomed me with open arms.

3: What unexpected joys or revelations have come from this process?

A: I learned to love me and discovered that I'm a pretty great individual. Through sharing my testimony, I learned that while I was struggling to find my identity, others in my life were inspired by my grit, honesty, vulnerability, and drive. I know that was God's hands, because I needed to learn to tap into these very things to experience healing.

4: Has this journey reshaped the way you define success or fulfillment? If so, how?

A: I didn't know who I was, so I conformed to what everyone else was doing. Once I started to really get to know God for myself, I continue to find contentment in Him. I can stand on His promises because I have seen what He has done in my life before and I know I will see it again and again.

5: What advice would you give someone in a similar rut?

A: First, be honest with yourself. Take accountability for your actions, pray for direction, and execute a plan. What do you want life to be like? Write the vision, no matter how big it is. Do the work. One of my favorite authors, Mark Batterson, says you have to work like it depends on you and pray like it depends on God.

Create Feedback Loops

Success is the sum of small efforts,

repeated day in and day out.

— ROBERT COLLIER

In the mid-1990s, as Pixar was struggling to get off the ground, one of its key early executives, Ed Catmull, was faced with a monumental challenge: how to foster creativity in an environment where failure was not only feared but actively avoided. He realized that the company's creative process would need more than just talented artists—it needed a culture of feedback, where team members could grow from criticism and adapt.

Catmull and his colleagues realized they needed a feedback loop, one that didn't just focus on the work but also on how individuals could grow from feedback themselves. This approach was unconventional in an industry that prized perfect products above all else, but Pixar's team learned to embrace the uncomfortable—dissecting their projects, seeking critique, and revising their approach to move forward. They didn't just make changes based on the feedback from others; they learned from each misstep to improve, growing stronger and more innovative with every round.

This concept of embracing feedback, not as a critique but as a tool for progress, aligns with the message of Proverbs 19:20: "Listen to advice and accept discipline, and at the end you will be counted among the wise." This principle doesn't just apply to teams but to each of us individually. We often give advice to others, yet when it comes to applying it to ourselves, we falter. Sometimes we fall into the trap of thinking we have all the answers, but wisdom comes when we realize that advice we give to others can be just as beneficial for us.

A feedback loop isn't just about listening to others; it's about listening to our own words too. If you constantly encourage others to push beyond their limits or take calculated risks but shy away from applying those same principles to your own life, you miss the opportunity for growth. This loop, when used properly, invites us to continually revisit our own advice, to act on it, and to refine ourselves through the process.

Psychologically, this feedback loop aligns with what is known as "self-directed learning." The research states that people who reflect on their actions, seek out feedback, and actively apply those insights are more likely to succeed long-term. It's not just about hearing what needs to be fixed—it's about being open to receiving that feedback, processing it, and then using it to make better decisions, just like Ed Catmull did with Pixar. By allowing ourselves to embrace both positive and constructive feedback, we position ourselves to improve in all areas of our lives, bringing us closer to who God has created us to be.

The next time you offer advice, take a moment to consider: *How can I apply this in my own life?* Revisit your words. Make sure the feedback loop is active, not only for others but for you too. It's through this process of reflecting, learning, and applying that we continue growing, just as Christ intends for us to.

Listen to advice and accept discipline, and at the end you will be counted among the wise.

— PROVERBS 19:20

LORD,
thank You for the wisdom that comes through feedback and reflection. Help me to be humble enough to receive both encouragement and correction, and give me the strength to act on what I learn. Teach me to see feedback as an opportunity to grow closer to the person You've created me to be.
AMEN.

QUESTIONS TO CONSIDER:

1. How do you typically respond to feedback, both positive and constructive?
2. Are there areas in your life where you've been resistant to advice or correction? Why?
3. What advice do you often give to others that you haven't yet applied in your own life?
4. How can you create intentional feedback loops in your personal or professional life?
5. How can embracing feedback help you grow spiritually and align with God's plan for your life?

RIGHT NOW:

- Reflect on a piece of advice or feedback you've recently received but haven't acted on. Write it down and consider why you've hesitated.
- Identify one area where you often give advice to others but haven't applied the same wisdom to yourself.

THIS WEEK:

- Seek feedback from one trusted person in your life about an area where you'd like to improve. Be intentional about listening without defensiveness.
- Write down one practical step you can take to act on that feedback, and put it into practice.

MOVING FORWARD:

- Establish a regular time for reflection, whether weekly or monthly, to evaluate your progress and revisit feedback you've received.
- Make it a habit to revisit advice you've given to others and apply it to your own life as needed.

Reminder:

Growth happens when you embrace feedback as an opportunity to refine, improve, and move closer to the person God has called you to be.

Gamify Your Goals

It's not just about winning a game;
it's about learning how to keep playing.
— JANE MCGONIGAL

In the gaming world, small victories keep players engaged. They earn points, unlock achievements, level up, and gain a constant sense of progress and motivation. Game designer and author of *Super Better* Jane McGonigal realized that these principles could be applied to everyday life. After a debilitating brain injury, she turned her recovery into a personal game, creating small challenges and celebrating each milestone. This approach transformed her healing journey, giving her the determination to move forward, even on the toughest days.

Gamifying your routine doesn't mean playing literal games all day. It's about turning mundane tasks or overwhelming goals into something engaging and rewarding. Want to reignite your passion for life? Break your day into mini-challenges and attach prizes to them. You'll create momentum and make even the most tedious tasks feel purposeful. Gamification taps into a deep psychological need for progress, mastery, and a sense of accomplishment. Additionally, studies in behavioral psychology indicate that rewards, progress tracking, and friendly competition improve productivity and morale.

Ecclesiastes 3:22 says, "There is nothing better for a person than to enjoy their work, because that is their lot." This Scripture reminds us that joy can be found in the ordinary moments. When you find ways to make your work enjoyable, you'll begin to embrace the gift of daily life and honor God in your efforts.

So, what can this look like in your daily routines? Doing the laundry becomes a race against the clock. Completing three items on your to-do list earns you a well-deserved break. Even cleaning your desk can feel like "leveling up" as you create a more organized space. The beauty of gamification is that it's customizable. You can set your own rules and rewards based on what motivates you. For example, if you're trying to pray more consistently, you might create a prayer calendar where each day completed adds to a visual chain of progress. Or, if your goal is to read the Bible, you could treat each completed chapter as a "level up" in your spiritual journey.

These simple shifts can help you stay consistent and even look forward to tasks that once felt like burdens. Gamification reminds us that life doesn't have to feel like a grind. By finding ways to make your routine enjoyable and rewarding, you're inviting both fun and purpose into your day. And as you celebrate each small victory, you're reminded that God delights in your progress, cheering you on as you continue to grow and serve Him. Each step forward—no matter how small—is worth celebrating.

What part of your routine could use a little gamification? Start small, get creative, and see how this playful approach can transform not just your tasks but your mindset.

So I saw that there is nothing better for a person than to enjoy their work, because that is their lot. For who can bring them to see what will happen after them?

— ECCLESIASTES 3:22

HEAVENLY FATHER,

thank You for the gift of each day and the opportunity to find joy in the small things. Help me to approach my daily tasks with creativity, energy, and a playful heart, knowing that even the smallest steps bring me closer to Your purpose for my life.

AMEN.

QUESTIONS TO CONSIDER:

1. What tasks in your daily routine feel the most overwhelming or monotonous?
2. How can you reframe these tasks to feel more engaging or rewarding?
3. What small victories could you celebrate today to create momentum for tomorrow?
4. How might gamifying your spiritual practices, like prayer or Bible reading, encourage you to stay consistent?
5. How can finding joy in your work honor God and His purpose for your life?

RIGHT NOW:

- Choose one task from your daily routine that feels like a chore. Think of one creative way to make it more engaging, such as setting a timer, adding music, or turning it into a small challenge.
- Reflect on one area of your life where you could celebrate small victories, like completing a to-do list or spending time with God.

THIS WEEK:

- Create a visual progress tracker for a specific goal, like a habit chain for consistent prayer or a points system for completing daily tasks.
- Assign small rewards for hitting milestones, such as a coffee break after completing a project or extra time doing something you enjoy after finishing a challenging task.

MOVING FORWARD:

- Integrate gamification into your broader goals. For example, treat each milestone on a large project as "leveling up" or create friendly competition by sharing your progress with a trusted friend or accountability partner.
- Reflect on how celebrating progress—not just results—helps you stay motivated and connected to God's purpose in your daily life.

Reminder:

Every small victory is worth celebrating because God delights in your progress and growth.

Schedule Nothing

To be alone by being part of everything—
this is the secret of solitude.
— THOMAS MERTON

There's a lot you can do to get out of your rut, but doing *nothing* is just as necessary.

Thomas Merton, a Trappist monk, spent much of his life seeking God in the stillness of nature. His journals, particularly *Zen and the Birds of Appetite* and *The Asian Journal of Thomas Merton*, reveal a man deeply committed to the practice of solitude. Merton often reflected on the importance of creating intentional moments of "nothingness"—time free from distractions, tasks, and noise—to connect with God and the world around him.

One of his most powerful realizations came during a trip to the mountains, where he simply sat in silence, observing the wind, the trees, and the interplay of light and shadow. In those moments, he discovered that scheduling nothing was not about emptiness but fullness—an opportunity to rediscover the divine in the ordinary. Merton's life reminds us that our most profound insights often come when we intentionally step away from the busyness of life.

Jesus Himself modeled this practice throughout His ministry. Luke 5:16 tells us, "Jesus often withdrew to lonely places and prayed." In the midst of teaching, healing, and leading, He intentionally made time to step away, not out of necessity but to reconnect with the Father. These moments of solitude were not wasted time; they were essential to His mission. If even the Son of God needed space to be still and refocus, how much more do we?

Today, when productivity is glorified and busyness is a badge of honor, the idea of scheduling nothing can feel countercultural. Yet downtime is critical for positive mental health, boosted creativity, and overall well-being. Neuroscientists have found that when our brains are at rest, they're still active—processing, reflecting, and making connections we might miss in the rush of activity. That's why these moments of "nothingness" allow us to quiet our hearts and hear God's still, small voice.

What would it look like to intentionally schedule nothing into your day? Perhaps it's five minutes of sitting in silence with a cup of tea, an hour-long walk without headphones, or an afternoon spent watching the clouds drift by. You're not being unproductive; you're being present and reawakening your appreciation for life.

Thomas Merton once wrote, "We cannot see things in perspective until we cease to hug them to our bosom." So, take a page from Merton's journals and Jesus' example. Let go of your need to control every moment. Set aside time to do nothing, and let that nothingness become an opportunity to encounter God in a deeper way. You might be surprised by what He reveals in the stillness.

Jesus often withdrew to lonely places and prayed.

— LUKE 5:16

LORD,
help me to embrace stillness and solitude.
Teach me to let go of busyness and distractions,
so I can hear Your voice and feel Your presence.
Fill the quiet moments with Your peace, wisdom,
and purpose.
AMEN.

QUESTIONS TO CONSIDER:

1. When was the last time you intentionally paused and did nothing?
2. How does busyness affect your ability to connect with God and yourself?
3. What fears or resistance come up when you think about scheduling time for stillness?
4. How might moments of quiet allow you to see God's presence in your daily life?
5. What does "doing nothing" look like for you, and how can it help you realign with God's purpose?

RIGHT NOW:

- Take five minutes to sit in silence, without distractions, and reflect on the presence of God in your life.
- Find a quiet spot, such as a corner of your home, a park bench, or even your car, and spend a moment simply observing your surroundings.

THIS WEEK:

- Block off fifteen minutes in your schedule for intentional stillness. Use this time to rest, reflect, and pray, leaving all distractions behind.
- Choose one daily task—like your commute, your morning coffee, or a walk—and do it without multitasking or noise, focusing instead on being present.

MOVING FORWARD:

- Make it a habit to schedule "nothing" regularly, whether it's weekly or even daily. Use this time to be still before God, reconnect with His purpose, and recharge your spirit.
- Begin keeping a journal to note what you experience, hear, or feel during these quiet moments over time.

Reminder:

Stillness is not a waste—it's where God meets you most profoundly.

Do Something Generous

No one has ever become poor by giving.

— ANNE FRANK

Hattie McDaniel, the first Black woman to win an Academy Award, knew the power of generosity. Despite facing discrimination in her career and personal life, McDaniel never allowed these barriers to harden her heart. She donated generously to educational causes, including the National Association for the Advancement of Colored People (NAACP) and scholarships for her sorority, Sigma Gamma Rho. McDaniel understood that her success was an opportunity to open doors for others. She appeared in more than three hundred films, had her own radio series, *Beulah*, and used her success to uplift others. Hattie McDaniel's generosity reminds us that giving isn't limited to money. It can be your time, your skills, or even your encouragement. Her life was a testament to how acts of generosity, both big and small, can ripple out to impact countless lives.

The beauty of generosity is that it doesn't require wealth or status—just a willingness to share what you have. The *Pay It Forward* movement, inspired by Catherine Ryan Hyde's novel of the same name, proves this. The concept of paying it forward is simple: Perform a generous act for someone without expecting anything in return, encouraging them to do the same for someone else. Whether it's paying for a stranger's coffee, offering a word of encouragement, or volunteering your time, these small acts create a chain of kindness that has the potential to change lives. Imagine the difference it could make if every person committed to one small act of generosity today. What starts as a single seed of kindness could grow into a forest of hope and love.

There's a reason Jesus tells us, "It is more blessed to give than to receive," in Acts 20:35. Being generous and giving freely allows us to not only bless others but experience the joy and fulfillment that come from living in alignment with God's character. Psychologists have observed that generosity activates areas of the brain associated with joy and connection. People who give—whether through time, money, or effort—often report higher levels of happiness and lower levels of stress.

Generosity opens our hearts to trust in God's provision and reminds us that everything we have ultimately comes from Him. Like Hattie McDaniel, you have something to give. It might not feel like much, and that's okay. Even the smallest acts of kindness can pull you out of this rut and have a lasting impact on your life. So, try mentoring someone, donating to a cause you care about, or simply offering a listening ear. Your generosity can inspire others to pay it forward.

Today, take a moment to reflect on how you can be generous. Remember, generosity isn't about the size of the gift but the heart behind it. As you step out in faith to bless others, you'll find that God's blessings pour back into your life in ways you never expected.

It is more blessed to give than to receive.

— ACTS 20:35

LORD,
thank You for blessing me with the ability to give.
Open my heart to see the needs around me and
give me the courage and compassion to act generously.
Let my acts of kindness reflect Your love and
inspire others to do the same.
AMEN.

QUESTIONS TO CONSIDER:

1. What resources or skills do you have that could bless someone else?
2. How can you practice generosity in nonmonetary ways this week?
3. Has there been a time when someone's generosity changed your life? How can you pay it forward?
4. What holds you back from being more generous?
5. How does giving without expecting anything in return shape your relationship with God?

RIGHT NOW:

- Perform one small act of kindness today. It could be sending an encouraging text, buying coffee for a stranger, or offering to help a friend.
- Take five minutes to reflect on one area of your life where you feel God is calling you to give, whether through time, skills, or resources.

THIS WEEK:

- Volunteer for a local cause, church event, or community project where your time and effort can make a difference.
- Identify three people in your life who could benefit from your encouragement or support, and take intentional action to uplift them.

MOVING FORWARD:

- Begin setting aside a small portion of your resources—whether financial or otherwise—to consistently support a cause or individual in need.
- Create a Generosity Journal to track the acts of kindness you've received and given, and reflect on how these moments impact your faith journey.

Reminder:

Generosity is less about what you give and more about the love and intention behind it.

Record Your Wins

I have not failed.
I've just found 10,000 ways that won't work.
— THOMAS EDISON

Have you ever dove into one of those enormous ball pits as a kid? If not, picture this: a bedroom-sized pool filled with colorful plastic balls. You leap in with joy, expecting laughter and fun, only to realize the balls are sticky, smelly, and hard. As you move, they shift unpredictably, and the more you struggle to climb out, the faster you sink deeper into the chaos.

Suddenly, it's dark. You're flailing, overwhelmed, and unsure which direction leads out. But then you remember: This isn't quicksand or deep waters. The ball pit can't *actually* trap you. Your air isn't running out. You're not drowning. You'll be fine. The key to escaping isn't thrashing and panicking, it's lifting your hand, waving it around, and trusting that someone's going to pull you out.

Life often feels like that ball pit. You leap into a dream or plan, but it doesn't turn out the way you'd hoped. Instead of joy, you find yourself buried under the weight of failures, disappointments, and unmet expectations. The more you try to fix things yourself, the more overwhelmed you feel.

But here's the thing: You don't have to claw your way out. God is there, waiting for you to lift your hand and call on Him. Psalm 40:2 says, "He lifted me out of the slimy pit, out of the mud and mire; He set my feet on a rock and gave me a firm place to stand." God is faithful, and His rescue isn't limited to your ability to fight your way out. He pulls you out of the pit because He loves you, not because you've earned it.

Life may feel like a chaotic, stinky pit right now, but you can find your way back to joy by trusting Him, and you can learn to trust Him by remembering. Think back to the times you've been in this place before—when the pit seemed too deep, and you felt too weak. Did you break? No. The God who held you then is the same God who holds you now. He's the God who turned impossible situations into blessings, who made a way when there was no way.

Take a moment to reflect on your past victories. Write them down, no matter how small they seem. How did you overcome a fear? What helped you find peace in the storm? Which closed door led to an unexpected blessing? Each victory is a testimony of God's faithfulness—a reminder that He has always been with you, and He always will.

Life's pits may feel overwhelming, but you're not alone in them. God is there, ready to pull you out, as He's done before. Lift your hand to Him, and trust His strength. When you pause to remember His past goodness, you'll find hope in His ability to guide you through today's struggles. The God who brought you through yesterday will carry you through today and tomorrow. Trust Him—you're going to be okay.

> **He lifted me out of the slimy pit, out of the mud and mire; He set my feet on a rock and gave me a firm place to stand.**
>
> — PSALM 40:2

LORD,
thank You for Your faithfulness in every season of my life. Help me to remember the times You've pulled me through the pits of fear, failure, and frustration. Remind me of Your steadfast love, and give me the courage to trust You again today.
AMEN.

QUESTIONS TO CONSIDER:

1. When was the last time God brought you out of a challenging situation?
2. How has reflecting on past victories helped you gain perspective in the present?
3. What does it mean to you that God's rescue doesn't depend on your own strength?
4. How can you practice gratitude for the small wins in your daily life?
5. What steps can you take to trust God in your current "pit" moment?

RIGHT NOW:

- Write down three specific times when God rescued you or brought you through a difficult situation. Reflect on how those moments demonstrated His faithfulness.
- Take a deep breath, lift a hand in prayer, and thank God for carrying you through past struggles.

THIS WEEK:

- Start a Win Journal where you record one victory each day, big or small. Whether it's finishing a task, finding peace in a tough moment, or extending kindness to someone, celebrate it as a sign of God's grace in your life.
- Share one of your testimonies with a friend, reminding them of God's goodness and encouraging them in their own journey.

MOVING FORWARD:

- At the end of each week, set aside time to review your Win Journal. Reflect on how God's faithfulness has been evident in both big and small ways.
- Memorize Psalm 40:2 as a reminder that no pit is too deep for God to pull you out.

Reminder:

You've overcome so much before, and the same God who carried you then is with you now. Lift your hand, trust His strength, and remember—you're going to be okay.

Measure Your Minutes

We all have the same twenty-four hours in a day.
The key is how we use them.
— UNKNOWN

Benjamin Franklin was the ultimate time management pioneer. While many of us are running through the endless hours of our day in a haze, Franklin had a simple but profound approach: He blocked out every moment. He tracked his time meticulously, asking himself each morning, "What good shall I do this day?"

Franklin's daily schedule wasn't a rigid to-do list; it was a blueprint for intentional living. His day began early, at five o'clock, with a few key activities to set the tone: wash up, breakfast, personal study, and preparation for work. He would spend the next three hours getting ready, mentally and physically, for the day ahead. From eight until noon, he focused solely on work—whether it was philosophy, science, or the development of his printing business. He spent four hours diving deeply into his tasks without distraction.

Franklin's midday routine was just as simple yet effective. After a morning of focused work, he would take a two-hour break to review his current projects and eat lunch, followed by a short time of reading. This reflection period ensured he stayed aligned with his goals. The afternoon was then dedicated to more focused work, another four hours of moving closer to his purpose. He closed the day with a four-hour evening of rest, reflection, and winding down. Franklin valued balance, and his evenings were for dinner and relaxation before preparing for another full day.

The most fascinating part? Franklin didn't do this to boast about his achievements. He simply knew that time was sacred—his time was a gift, and he needed to steward it wisely. In doing so, he ensured his life was one of clarity, growth, and service. Because of his time management and focus, we now have access to his revolutionary inventions: bifocals, swim fins, the lightning rod, and more!

We all have twenty-four hours in a day, and just like Franklin, our time is a gift from God. Ephesians 5:15–16 reminds us to "be very careful, then, how you live—not as unwise but as wise, making the most of every opportunity." How many opportunities are you leaving on the table simply because you haven't paid attention to where your time goes?

Maybe you're in a rut because you're letting distractions steal hours of potentially productive time. Maybe your time for learning is being robbed by TV, gossip, or overthinking. Or maybe your time isn't aligned with your calling. What would your life look like if you took Franklin's approach, choosing to make each moment intentional?

Time is one of the few resources we can't get back. The days may pass by slowly, but years fly by in the blink of an eye, leaving behind either accomplishments or regrets but never indifference. So, what will you do with the time you've been given?

Be very careful, then, how you live—not as unwise but as wise, making the most of every opportunity.

— EPHESIANS 5:15–16

LORD,

thank You for the gift of time. Teach me to steward it wisely, aligning my days with Your purpose. Help me to see opportunities where I can grow, serve, and glorify You. Show me how to use my time in ways that bring honor to You and peace to my life.

AMEN.

QUESTIONS TO CONSIDER:

1. How often do you reflect on how you're spending time?
2. Are your daily activities aligned with your long-term goals and God's calling on your life?
3. What distractions most often steal your time, and how can you address them?
4. How can you incorporate intentional rest and reflection into your routine?
5. What's one way you can honor God with your time this week?

RIGHT NOW:

- Take fifteen minutes to write down how you've spent your time over the past twenty-four hours. Be honest and include everything, from work to social media scrolling to rest.
- Reflect on your list and identify any patterns or distractions that may be preventing you from using your time wisely.

THIS WEEK:

- Create a simple daily schedule that includes time for focused work, rest, and prayer. Try blocking out chunks of time for specific activities, just as Benjamin Franklin did.
- Set a timer during work or study sessions to stay on track and minimize distractions.

MOVING FORWARD:

- At the end of each week, review how you spent your time. Celebrate where you stayed aligned with your goals, and identify areas for improvement.
- Begin each morning by asking Franklin's guiding question: "What good shall I do this day?" Use it as a prompt to align your actions with God's purpose for you.

Reminder:

Time is sacred. Use it wisely, for every moment is an opportunity to honor God and move closer to your calling.

"Emotions are signals, not facts that define us."

INTERVIEW 2:

Identity After Motherhood

BY: NICOLE WOODCOX BOLDEN
LICENSED CLINICAL
SOCIAL WORKER | DOULA

1: What are you reigniting, reawakening, rediscovering, or reclaiming in this season?

A: I am reclaiming my God-given identity, one that honors my authentic self. Becoming a mother shook me to my core, as I battled severe postpartum depression and anxiety while navigating the overwhelming expectations of motherhood. I lost myself in societal "shoulds," a cloud that lingered for years. My turning point came when I realized I couldn't fully support my eldest daughter in embracing her identity while I was still unsure of my own. This journey has been about reclaiming clarity, confidence, and authenticity for us both.

2: What challenges have you faced in this process and what have they taught you?

A: My biggest challenge has been releasing the coping mechanism of people-pleasing. Saying "no" more often to create intentional space for self-care felt uncomfortable. I value being a kind, safe presence, and this shift made me question my values. But, through prayer and reflection, I realized that people-pleasing is rooted in fear, not love—and it doesn't align with the person I'm becoming. This season reminded me that God can use all things for His good when we're open to His guidance. I realized my season of depression was actually His invitation to evolve into a more connected version of myself, and that emotions are signals, not facts that define us.

3: What unexpected joys or revelations have come from this process?

A: This season revealed that I hadn't just lost my identity, I'd lost trust in myself. The unexpected joy came from embracing the spiritual gifts God has given me, gifts I once dismissed as ordinary. I've come to fully recognize my power to do the work He has called me to do.

4: Has this journey reshaped the way you define success or fulfillment? If so, how?

A: I used to define success through self-sacrifice and simply meeting goals. Now, success means staying emotionally connected to myself, growth, and having a positive impact on the people that I meet along the journey.

5: What advice would you give someone who feels stuck in a similar rut?

A: Practice holistic gratitude, not toxic positivity. This is the ability to zoom out and see the bigger picture, including the support around you. Sometimes these seasons teach us how to receive. Take intentional time to reflect on what your emotions might be inviting you to explore.

Unleash Your Dreams

It's kind of fun to do the impossible.

— WALT DISNEY

When we think about creativity, we often limit ourselves. We put boundaries on what's possible because we're afraid of the unknown or skeptical about our ideas. But Joel 2:28 says, "I will pour out My Spirit on all people. Your sons and daughters will prophesy, your old men will dream dreams, your young men will see visions," reminding us that God has given us the ability to see beyond the limits of this world. Whether we're young or old, He stirs visions and dreams within us.

Walt Disney, a master of imagination, is a perfect example of how this biblical truth plays out in real lives. By embracing the impossible, he revolutionized entertainment. Disney's philosophy was simple: Think big and dream without boundaries. "It's kind of fun to do the impossible," he famously said, and his company built an empire on that principle. He believed in creating experiences that would spark awe and inspiration in the hearts of people everywhere.

Disney's creative process, which became known as "Disney's Creative Strategy" in 1994, is an example of how dreams can be translated into reality. Neuro-Linguistic Programming (NLP) expert Robert Dilts identified three key phases in this process: the Dreamer, the Realist, and the Critic. Each phase is necessary for turning visionary ideas into practical plans—first by dreaming without limits, then by figuring out how to make it work, and finally by critiquing to ensure success.

Joel's prophecy speaks to a truth we can all probably relate to: The older we get, the more our dreams deepen. The visions we once had may evolve, but they'll never completely disappear.

It's easy to get caught up in the day-to-day grind, dismissing our wild ideas because they seem too far out there, or because the timing isn't right. But what if, instead trying to make our dreams fit into safe boxes, we let them grow without restrictions? What if we fully embraced the possibility that the impossible is just a dream waiting to come alive?

Instead of fearing the unknown or what others think, we are called to lean into the creativity that God has planted within us. The good news is, we don't have to create by our own power. When we partner with God in our creativity, He opens doors and connects dots we couldn't even begin to imagine. When we stop limiting ourselves, we give Him the space to work wonders through us.

Remember, every great biblical story started with someone daring to believe in what seemed impossible—Noah building an ark, Moses confronting Pharaoh, David facing Goliath. Your dreams, anchored in faith, can have the same world-changing potential.

So today, I invite you to embrace your visions. Whether you're just starting out or looking to dream again, remember that with God, there are no limits. Like Walt Disney, who built a world out of imagination, you, too, can build the future that's in your heart.

> **I will pour out My Spirit on all people. Your sons and daughters will prophesy, your old men will dream dreams, your young men will see visions.**
>
> — JOEL 2:28

FATHER,

thank You for the gift of dreams and visions.

Help me to embrace the creativity and imagination

You have placed within me. Give me courage to pursue

the impossible, knowing that with You, all things are possible.

Guide my steps and align my dreams with Your purpose for my life.

AMEN.

QUESTIONS TO CONSIDER:

1. What dreams or ideas have you put aside because they seemed too big or impossible?
2. How does Joel 2:28 encourage you to view your dreams differently?
3. In what areas of your life have you been afraid to step out and embrace creativity?
4. How can you partner with God to bring your dreams to life?
5. Who in your life inspires you to think big and believe in the impossible?

RIGHT NOW:

- Take ten minutes to write down your wildest dreams without judgment or limitations. Let your imagination flow freely, listing every idea, big or small.
- Reflect on Joel 2:28 and ask God to reveal which dreams He wants you to pursue.

THIS WEEK:

- Identify one dream from your list that excites you the most. Break it into smaller, actionable steps using Disney's Creative Strategy:
    - Dreamer: What's the ultimate vision?
    - Realist: What practical steps can you take to begin?
    - Critic: What challenges might arise, and how can you address them?
- Share your dream with a trusted friend or mentor for encouragement and support.

MOVING FORWARD:

- Dedicate time each week to revisiting your dreams and progress. Use this as a moment to pray, reflect, and ask God for direction.
- Document small wins and breakthroughs as a way to build momentum and remind yourself of God's faithfulness.

Reminder:

Your dreams are seeds of possibility planted by God. When you embrace them with faith, there are no limits to what He can do through you.

Set Your Triggers

Stormy or sunny days, glorious or lonely nights,
I maintain an attitude of gratitude.
— MAYA ANGELOU

Anne Lamott once said, "Gratitude begins in our hearts and then dovetails into behavior. It almost always makes you willing to be of service, which is where the joy resides." Gratitude isn't just an emotion—it's an action. It transforms how we see our lives and engages us to live out our faith in real, tangible ways.

Lamott, a celebrated author known for her raw honesty and humor, recounts how gratitude saved her during some of her darkest seasons. As she wrestled with addiction, grief, and self-doubt, she began to practice intentional thankfulness for the smallest things—a warm cup of coffee, a friend's phone call, moments of silence. These daily acknowledgments of grace pulled her back from despair and reminded her of God's abiding presence in the ordinary.

Gratitude, as Lamott teaches, is not a passive response to good fortune but a deliberate choice to see the fingerprints of God in every aspect of life. Colossians 3:17 encourages this mindset, urging us to do everything—every word and deed—in the name of Jesus, giving thanks to God.

Think about your own day. How often do you pause to say thank You to God? It's easy to express gratitude during mountaintop moments—a promotion at work, a milestone celebration, or a prayer answered in the way you hoped. But what about the valleys and plateaus of life? What about the endless emails that prove you're needed and thought of, the piles of laundry that you get to wash and wear, or the car that always needs gas because you live an eventful, full life? These, too, are sacred opportunities for gratitude.

Setting gratitude triggers is a great way to pull yourself out of an emotional rut. The idea of a "gratitude trigger" is to attach thankfulness to the small, recurring aspects of your daily life. For instance, you could pause for a moment of gratitude every time you pour your morning coffee, every time you step into your car, or even when you wash your hands. These triggers remind you to look for God's grace in the ordinary. Over time, this practice becomes second nature, shifting your focus from what's lacking to what's already abundant.

Gratitude, like a muscle, grows stronger with use. The more you practice it, the more it shapes your perspective, making even the most routine tasks feel like acts of worship. You may start to notice the beauty in overlooked places—a ray of sunlight through your kitchen window, the sound of laughter in the background, or even the rhythm of your heartbeat.

Anne Lamott discovered the joy that comes from gratitude not just in her triumphs but in her struggles. Her practice of thankfulness became a lifeline, connecting her to the God who is always near, and her journey shows us that gratitude is not about denying pain or pretending life is perfect. It's about choosing to see God's goodness in the midst of it all.

Whatever you do, whether in word or deed, do it all in the name of the Lord Jesus, giving thanks to God the Father through Him.

— COLOSSIANS 3:17

LORD,

thank You for the countless blessings You provide each day. Teach me to see Your grace in the ordinary and to cultivate a heart of gratitude no matter the season. Help me to pause and acknowledge Your goodness, transforming even the smallest moments into acts of worship.

AMEN.

QUESTIONS TO CONSIDER:

1. What are some small, recurring moments in your day where you can intentionally pause to thank God?
2. How does gratitude help you recognize God's presence in the mundane parts of life?
3. In what ways can practicing gratitude reshape how you approach challenging situations?
4. Are there overlooked blessings in your daily life that you've taken for granted?
5. How can you make gratitude a consistent part of your routine?

RIGHT NOW:

- Identify three daily activities or moments (e.g., pouring coffee, starting your car, brushing your teeth) that you can use as gratitude triggers. Write them down.
- Pause during one of those activities today to thank God for specific blessings in your life.

THIS WEEK:

- Each day, intentionally practice your gratitude triggers during the moments you've identified. Take a deep breath, pause, and thank God for one thing in that moment.
- Keep a journal to write down at least three things you're thankful for each evening. This practice will help reinforce a mindset of gratitude.

MOVING FORWARD:

- Incorporate gratitude into your prayer life by beginning each prayer with a list of things you're thankful for, no matter how small.
- Share your gratitude with others by expressing thanks to those who have positively impacted your life, whether through a note, a call, or a simple conversation.

Reminder:
Gratitude turns ordinary moments into extraordinary reminders of God's goodness.

Shape Your Space

The successful warrior is the average man,
with laser-like focus.
— BRUCE LEE

The constant pull of distractions has a quiet way of derailing us. These distractions don't always announce themselves with loud alerts or glaring lights—sometimes they slip in unnoticed, cluttering our thoughts and fragmenting our focus. Walter Dill Scott, an early pioneer in industrial psychology, recognized the impact of distractions on productivity. Through his groundbreaking work in the early 1900s, he demonstrated how simple, intentional changes—like grouping similar tasks together or organizing physical spaces—could lead to remarkable improvements in clarity and efficiency.

Scott's insights remain strikingly relevant today. Notifications chime endlessly, calendars overflow with obligations, and a steady hum of mental clutter competes for our attention. The more we try to keep up, the more scattered we become. Focus isn't achieved by doing more or trying harder; it's found in stripping away what doesn't belong.

Hebrews 12:1–2 gives us a roadmap: "Let us throw off everything that hinders and the sin that so easily entangles. And let us run with perseverance the race marked out for us, fixing our eyes on Jesus, the pioneer and perfecter of faith." This Scripture isn't just about clearing external distractions but also shedding the internal burdens—fear, doubt, worry—that hold us back from fully embracing God's calling.

Jesus often modeled this principle during His time on Earth. Faced with the demands of ministry, He withdrew to solitary places to pray, carving out intentional moments to connect with the Father. He wasn't consumed by every need or opportunity but remained focused on His divine purpose. His example reminds us that creating space isn't a luxury; it's essential for aligning ourselves with God's plan.

Take a moment to consider the clutter in your own life. It's not always about physical mess—though that can be part of it. It might be an overloaded schedule, the pressure of unrealistic expectations, or the endless scroll of social media. These distractions pull us in many directions, but none lead us closer to God's purpose.

Clearing distractions is an act of faith. It's trusting that when we let go of what's unnecessary, we make room for what's truly important: opening space for God to move. When you intentionally remove what's holding you back, you'll find clarity, peace, and a renewed ability to run the race He has marked out for you.

Walter Dill Scott's simple methods of focus taught workers to organize their spaces for productivity, but they also carry a deeper truth: Creating order clears the way for purpose. By following his example and embracing the wisdom of Scripture, you can regain focus, align your priorities, and fix your eyes on the path God has set before you.

> **Let us throw off everything that hinders and the sin that so easily entangles. And let us run with perseverance the race marked out for us, fixing our eyes on Jesus, the pioneer and perfecter of faith.**
>
> — HEBREWS 12:1–2

LORD,

help me to clear the distractions that pull me away from Your purpose for my life. Teach me to recognize what hinders my focus and to create a space where Your presence and peace can dwell. Thank You for guiding me as I align my priorities with Your plan.

AMEN.

QUESTIONS TO CONSIDER:

1. What distractions are pulling your attention away from God's calling?
2. How does physical or mental clutter affect your ability to focus on what truly matters?
3. In what ways can creating order in your life help you hear God's voice more clearly?
4. Are there specific fears, doubts, or worries entangling you that need to be released?
5. How can you create intentional moments of solitude to connect with God in your daily routine?

RIGHT NOW:

- Identify one area of clutter in your life, whether it's your workspace, your schedule, or your mental state. Choose one small step to clear or organize it today.
- Set aside five minutes to pray and ask God to reveal any internal distractions that are weighing on you.

THIS WEEK:

- Dedicate thirty minutes to decluttering a physical space where you spend a lot of time (e.g., your desk, car, or a corner of your home). Reflect on how this impacts your focus.
- Practice limiting one source of distraction for a week, such as reducing social media usage or turning off unnecessary notifications.

MOVING FORWARD:

- Create a "focus space" for prayer, reflection, or work. This could be a small corner of a room or even a specific time of day set aside for quiet connection with God.
- Build a habit of ending each day by reviewing what aligned with your purpose and what needs adjustment.

Reminder:
Clearing space creates room for clarity, peace, and God's presence.

Release Your Regrets

We are products of our past,
but we don't have to be prisoners of it.
— RICK WARREN

In 2012 a palliative care nurse named Bronnie Ware published a book based on her years of listening to people at the end of their lives. Titled *The Top Five Regrets of the Dying*, it revealed common themes from her patients' reflections. They wished they had lived truer to themselves, worked less, expressed their feelings, stayed connected to loved ones, and allowed themselves to be happier. These regrets weren't just admissions of pain—they were lessons for those still living.

Regret is a universal experience. Whether it's a missed opportunity, a broken relationship, or a bad decision, we've all looked back and thought, *If only I had done things differently.* The apostle Paul writes in II Corinthians 7:10, "Godly sorrow brings repentance that leads to salvation and leaves no regret, but worldly sorrow brings death." This verse highlights a crucial distinction: While worldly sorrow keeps you stuck in shame, godly sorrow invites you to grow. Regret isn't meant to paralyze you. It's meant to propel you.

Think about a time when regret weighed heavily on your heart. Maybe you let fear stop you from pursuing a dream. Maybe you said words you can't take back or stayed silent when you should have spoken up. Whatever it was, remember this: Your past mistakes don't define you. God does. And He specializes in turning pain into purpose.

Joseph's story in the Bible is a powerful example. Sold into slavery by his brothers and falsely accused, Joseph endured years of hardship. Yet he didn't let bitterness take root. Instead, he trusted God's plan, and in time his trials became the foundation for a greater purpose—saving countless lives during a famine.

Your mistakes can serve a similar purpose. Start by facing them honestly. What are the top five things you wish you could go back and change? Write them down, not to dwell on the hurt but to examine what they reveal about your heart and priorities.

For instance, if you regret working too much and missing time with your family, that's a sign to realign your focus moving forward. If you regret not taking better care of your health, let it inspire you to make small, consistent changes today. Each regret carries a lesson—one that God can use to transform your future.

Jesus didn't come to erase the past; He came to redeem it. When you surrender your regrets to Him, He takes the broken pieces and shapes them into something spectacular. You're not defined by your failures, and you're not doomed to repeat them. You are a new creation in Christ, equipped to move forward with grace, wisdom, and hope.

Your regrets and mistakes are not the end of the story. With God, they are the beginning of a new chapter—one where pain becomes purpose, and sorrow gives way to joy.

Godly sorrow brings repentance that leads to salvation and leaves no regret, but worldly sorrow brings death.

— II CORINTHIANS 7:10

HEAVENLY FATHER,

thank You for Your endless grace and for the redemption You offer through Jesus. Help me to release my regrets and learn the lessons You have for me. Turn my sorrow into wisdom and my pain into purpose. Guide me as I move forward, trusting in Your plan for my life.

AMEN.

QUESTIONS TO CONSIDER:

1. What regrets have been weighing on your heart, and how have they shaped your perspective?
2. Are there patterns in your regrets that reveal areas God may be asking you to change or grow?
3. How has God already redeemed parts of your past that once felt broken?
4. What would it look like to let go of shame and embrace godly sorrow that leads to growth?
5. How can you use the lessons from your regrets to align your future choices with God's purpose?

RIGHT NOW:

- Take a quiet moment to reflect on the regrets you've been carrying. Write down the top five without judgment, focusing on what they reveal about your priorities and values.
- Pray over your list, asking God to help you release each regret into His hands and to reveal the lessons He wants you to learn.

THIS WEEK:

- Identify one regret that points to an area needing realignment in your life. Create a small, actionable step to move forward. For example, if you regret missed time with loved ones, plan a meaningful activity with them this week.
- Spend ten minutes each day meditating on II Corinthians 7:10, asking God to guide you toward repentance and growth rather than shame.

MOVING FORWARD:

- Regularly revisit your regrets, not to dwell on them but to track how God has used them to shape your journey. Write down moments of redemption and growth as reminders of His faithfulness.
- Create a new habit of checking in with yourself at the end of each week: Are you living in alignment with your values, or are you creating new regrets?

Reminder:

Your regrets are not the end of the story. God redeems, transforms, and uses every piece of your past to shape a brighter, purposeful future.

Anchor Yourself

The secret of your future is hidden in your daily routine.

— MIKE MURDOCK

In the early 1900s, Ivy Lee, a productivity consultant, introduced a game-changing principle to Bethlehem Steel's president, Charles M. Schwab: the power of a consistent routine. By prioritizing and structuring each day, Lee helped Schwab and his team revolutionize their efficiency. It was a simple concept, but its impact was transformative, proving that small, deliberate actions can create stability and focus.

Routines act as anchors, grounding us amidst the chaos of life. Psalm 5:3 captures this rhythm, saying, "In the morning, LORD, You hear my voice; in the morning I lay my requests before You and wait expectantly." The psalmist's daily habit of seeking God reminds us that routines aren't just about productivity—they're about centering ourselves in His presence and preparing our hearts to face the day.

Today, everything moves fast and demands are endless, and our lives can feel rushed, leaving us vulnerable to stress and burnout. But when we create regular, intentional spaces to reflect, pray, and connect with God, we ground ourselves in His grace, allowing Him to lead our thoughts and actions.

Jesus modeled this practice time and again. Before major decisions or after long days of ministry, He withdrew to pray and be with the Father. These moments of solitude weren't incidental; they were essential. They recharged His spirit and realigned Him with God's will.

Your day might feel too busy or unpredictable to imagine implementing a rhythm like this, but even small moments with God can have a profound impact. Whether it's the first thought you bring to Him in the morning or a quiet reflection on His faithfulness at night, these practices remind you that God is your ultimate source of strength and guidance.

Even modern science affirms the value of this kind of spiritual intentionality. Findings prove that consistent morning and evening habits can significantly enhance emotional well-being, focus, and resilience. But the benefits extend far beyond personal health. Spiritual routines prepare your heart to see God's hand in your day and respond to His call with clarity and peace.

What might it look like for you to anchor your days in Him? It doesn't have to be extravagant—a simple moment of gratitude, a short prayer, or sitting in stillness with Scripture can change the tone of your entire day. The key is consistency. The more you turn to God in the small moments, the more you'll find His presence guiding you in the big ones.

Life will always bring distractions, but deliberate routines help you resist the drift. When you make space for God in your daily rhythm, you'll discover not only focus and peace but the strength to navigate challenges and the joy of walking in step with Him.

In the morning, LORD, You hear my voice; in the morning I lay my requests before You and wait expectantly.

— PSALM 5:3

LORD,
help me create daily rhythms that draw me closer to You. Show me how to prioritize my time and center my day on Your presence. Give me the discipline to seek You consistently, trusting that in the stillness, You will meet me and guide my path.
AMEN.

QUESTIONS TO CONSIDER:

1. What does your current daily routine reveal about your priorities?
2. How often do you intentionally set aside time to connect with God each day?
3. What small, consistent action could you incorporate into your mornings or evenings to anchor yourself in God's presence?
4. How can rhythms of prayer, reflection, or stillness help you better handle stress or uncertainty?
5. In what ways has God shown up for you when you've made time for Him in the past?

RIGHT NOW:

- Spend five minutes reflecting on your current daily schedule. Write down when and where you feel most connected to God and when you feel distant or overwhelmed.
- Identify one specific time of day—morning, midday, or evening—when you can dedicate even two minutes to stillness, prayer, or Scripture.

THIS WEEK:

- Test a small habit to anchor your rhythm. For example, pray as soon as you wake up, or read a short Scripture before bed. Track how this affects your mood, focus, or connection with God.
- Choose a specific verse, such as Psalm 5:3, to meditate on each morning. Write it down somewhere visible to remind you to begin your day with Him.

MOVING FORWARD:

- Create a simple, repeatable routine that works for you. It could include a mix of prayer, journaling, and gratitude, even if it's just five to ten minutes daily.
- Revisit and refine your rhythm at the end of each month. What worked? What didn't? Adjust your practices as needed, always prioritizing God's presence in your life.

Reminder:

Daily rhythms aren't about perfection—they're about building a life anchored in God's presence, one small, faithful step at a time.

Find the Light

Joy does not simply happen to us.
We have to choose joy and keep choosing it every day.
— HENRI NOUWEN

Think back to a moment when you felt fully alive—a time when joy wasn't just a fleeting emotion but a tangible presence. Maybe it was while laughing with a close friend, standing in awe of a breathtaking view, or completing a project that filled you with pride. Whatever it was, that moment was more than just a memory; it was a glimpse of what God designed you for.

In Galatians 5:22–23, Paul writes about the fruit of the Spirit, with joy being one virtue of it. But how often do we pause to examine where joy is truly present in our lives? We tend to focus on what's wrong, what's missing, or what's next, leaving little room to appreciate the moments when God's goodness breaks through the noise.

There's a story about a psychologist named Dr. Martin Seligman, often referred to as the father of positive psychology. His research showed that reflecting on moments of joy not only improves mental health but also rewires the brain for positivity. The more you seek joy, the more you'll find it. One of his experiments involved asking participants to write down daily moments of happiness, no matter how small. The result? Increased levels of life satisfaction, even months after the exercise.

Take a moment to think about your own life. What are the patterns in your joy? Are there certain people, places, or activities that consistently fill your heart? Maybe it's a quiet morning spent in prayer, a walk in nature, or time spent creating something meaningful. These moments are markers of God's presence in your life.

But let's also acknowledge the flip side. Joy isn't always easy to access, especially in seasons of struggle. Even then, the discipline of noticing and naming joy is a form of resistance against despair. It's a way of saying, "God, I see You, even here."

Jesus Himself modeled this. In John 15:11 He tells His disciples, "I have told you this so that My joy may be in you and that your joy may be complete." His joy wasn't dependent on circumstances but rooted in obedience to the Father and a deep understanding of His purpose.

Your moments of joy are invitations to remember God's faithfulness. By reflecting on them, you train your heart to see His hand more clearly—not just in the mountaintop experiences but in the everyday blessings too.

Joy is a choice, but it's also a practice. The more you search for it, the more you'll find it, and the more you'll experience the fullness of life God promises.

The fruit of the Spirit is love, joy, peace, forbearance, kindness, goodness, faithfulness, gentleness and self-control.

— GALATIANS 5:22–23

LORD,

thank You for the gift of joy, even in the midst of life's challenges. Help me to see Your hand in the small, everyday blessings and to choose joy as a reflection of Your faithfulness. Open my heart to the fullness of life You promise, and teach me to carry Your joy wherever I go.

AMEN.

QUESTIONS TO CONSIDER:

1. What specific moments in your life have brought you lasting joy?
2. How can you intentionally make space for more joy in your daily routine?
3. In what ways has God revealed His faithfulness to you through joyful moments?
4. Are there patterns or habits that drain your joy? How can you address them?
5. How does reflecting on past joy help you trust God in seasons of difficulty?

RIGHT NOW:

- Write down three recent moments of joy, no matter how small. Reflect on what these moments reveal about God's presence and faithfulness in your life.
- Spend five minutes in silence, asking God to show you where joy is already present in your current season.

THIS WEEK:

- Start a Joy Journal where you write one thing each day that brought you joy. It could be as simple as a kind word, a moment of peace, or a beautiful sunset.
- Identify a person, place, or activity that consistently brings you joy and plan time to reconnect with it this week.

MOVING FORWARD:

- Look for opportunities to bring joy to others. This might be through a kind gesture, a thoughtful note, or an unexpected act of service. Often, sharing joy multiplies it.
- Revisit your Joy Journal regularly, especially during difficult times, as a reminder of God's goodness and faithfulness.

Reminder:

Joy isn't something you wait for; it's something you choose and cultivate. Train your heart to see God's goodness, and His joy will fill every corner of your life.

"Success is
about accepting
God's plan."

INTERVIEW 3:

Rediscovering Forgiveness After

BY: SHANETTA (NETTA) DINGLE
BIRTH & POSTPARTUM DOULA

1: What are you reigniting, reawakening, rediscovering, or reclaiming in this season?

A: After years of shame and unresolved sadness over my mother's passing, I'm finally finding peace and forgiveness for myself. A spiritual fast sparked this journey, and God instructed me to let her go. It's been about using faith and surrender to achieve healing.

2: What challenges have you faced in this process, and what have they taught you?

A: The challenges that I have faced through this process were emotional dysregulation at its best. I would be so angry and frustrated with anyone around me during a certain time of the year, which is November through January. I have worked through this with the power of prayer, meditation on God's Word, and mindfulness meditation as a daily routine.

Through this season, I have learned that God is bigger, and I take heed that His presence is powerful at the mention of His name. God comes to those who seek Him diligently (Psalm 145:18–19) in His presence. I prayed for God to deliver me from whatever was binding me, and He delivered me from the grief that I held on to for so long.

3: What unexpected joys or revelations have come from this process?

A: I had no idea how much weight I was carrying until I let go of the guilt. I found that my mother's love simply shifted but never left. Instead of sinking in sorrow, I now am most grateful for her light, which has given me a sense of joy, and I have learned to heal for the peace that I yearned for over ten years.

4: Has this journey reshaped the way you define success or fulfillment? If so, how?

A: Yes, definitely. Right now, success is about accepting God's plan, finding calm in acceptance, and honoring love rather than holding onto grief. It is no longer about control or fixing problems. Being grateful and appreciating what you have left is the path to contentment.

5: What advice would you give someone who feels stuck in a similar rut?

A: Let go and let God. I understand it's difficult to let go of the hurt and guilt, but remember that God is with you no matter what. Trust His plan and put it in His hands. Love yourself with kindness; you've done the best you can.

Write Permission Slips

Freedom lies in being bold.

— ROBERT FROST

In 2013 a renowned researcher and storyteller, Brené Brown, introduced an idea in her work about courage and vulnerability: the concept of "permission slips." While attending a meeting that left her feeling overwhelmed, she scribbled a note to herself: *"I give myself permission to feel anxious."* That small, intentional act shifted her perspective, giving her space to embrace her emotions without judgment.

It's a concept that resonates with Galatians 5:1, which reminds us, "It is for freedom that Christ has set us free. Stand firm, then, and do not let yourselves be burdened again by a yoke of slavery." While Paul speaks about spiritual freedom, the message holds true for our inner struggles as well. Too often, we imprison ourselves with the weight of perfectionism, fear of failure, or the endless need for approval.

Writing a permission slip—literally or figuratively—isn't about excusing poor behavior or settling for less. It's about creating space for grace, growth, and the boldness to try

And as we touched on previously, history gives us another powerful example of this principle through Thomas Edison. When working on the invention of the light bulb, Edison reportedly failed thousands of times before finding the right filament. When asked about his failures, he famously said, "I have not failed. I've just found ten thousand ways that won't work." Edison didn't need permission from anyone else to fail and keep trying—he gave it to himself.

Think about the areas in your life where fear might be holding you back. Is there a dream you've tucked away because you're afraid of what others might think? A calling you've delayed pursuing because you don't feel "ready"? God didn't create you to live in a cage of self-doubt. His Spirit equips you with freedom and boldness.

Giving yourself permission doesn't mean the process will be easy or without risk. But it shifts the focus from avoiding failure to embracing the lessons and opportunities each step offers. After all, growth happens when we allow ourselves to step into the unknown, trusting that God will meet us there.

Jesus often encouraged this kind of freedom in His disciples. When Peter stepped out of the boat to walk on water, he didn't wait for perfect conditions or absolute certainty. He acted on faith, trusting in Jesus' call. Yes, Peter faltered, but even then, Jesus reached out to steady him.

The same God who called Peter is calling you—to be bold, to take risks, and to trust that even in failure, He is working for your good.

Freedom begins with a decision: to release yourself from the pressure of perfection and embrace the grace God freely gives.

It is for freedom that Christ has set us free. Stand firm, then, and do not let yourselves be burdened again by a yoke of slavery.

— GALATIANS 5:1

LORD,

thank You for the freedom You've given me through Christ. Help me to release the burdens of perfectionism, fear, and self-doubt. Teach me to trust in Your grace as I step boldly into the plans You have for me. May I find courage in Your promises and the strength to move forward with faith. Amen.

QUESTIONS TO CONSIDER:

1. What areas of your life feel weighed down by fear or perfectionism?
2. Is there a dream or calling you've delayed pursuing because you feel unprepared or unworthy?
3. How can giving yourself permission to fail make room for God's grace to work in your life?
4. What would stepping into freedom look like in your current season?
5. How has God already shown you His faithfulness in moments when you took a risk or stepped out in faith?

RIGHT NOW:

- Write a literal permission slip to yourself. It could say, "I give myself permission to try and fail," "I give myself permission to rest without guilt," or "I give myself permission to start small." Keep it where you can see it as a daily reminder.
- Take five minutes to reflect on a fear that's been holding you back. Pray and ask God for courage to release that fear and trust Him with the outcome.

THIS WEEK:

- Identify one area where you've been holding yourself back, and take a small step forward. Whether it's signing up for a class, sharing your dream with a trusted friend, or starting a project, act in faith.
- Journal about a time when God turned what you thought was a failure into something meaningful. Reflect on how that experience shaped you.

MOVING FORWARD:

- Make it a habit to write permission slips for yourself whenever self-doubt creeps in. Whether it's weekly or as needed, remind yourself of the freedom God has already given you.
- Create a Boldness Journal to track the risks you take, the lessons you learn, and the ways God shows up in the process.

Reminder:

You are free to try, free to fail, and free to grow because God's grace is bigger than your fears. Step into that freedom boldly.

Choose Your Council

Surround yourself with only people who are going to lift you higher.

— OPRAH WINFREY

In 1776 Benjamin Franklin sat down with a group of like-minded individuals to form what would become known as the Junto Club. This group of thinkers, inventors, and leaders met regularly to discuss ideas, solve problems, and encourage one another toward personal and professional growth. Franklin knew that the company you keep can either propel you toward your purpose or pull you away from it.

Proverbs 15:22 says, "Plans fail for lack of counsel, but with many advisers they succeed." Scripture underscores the importance of surrounding yourself with wise and trusted voices—those who can offer guidance, encouragement, and accountability. These people act as your "Board of Directors," helping you navigate life's challenges and decisions.

Today this principle is mirrored in leadership and personal development circles. Researchers have found that mentorship and peer support significantly increase an individual's ability to achieve their goals. Studies from organizations like Harvard Business Review reveal that having a network of trusted advisors doesn't just improve success rates—it also boosts resilience and reduces burnout.

But here's the catch: Not every voice in your life deserves a seat at the table. Franklin's Junto Club wasn't open to everyone. He intentionally chose people who shared his values and were committed to growth.

Similarly, your Board of Directors should consist of individuals who reflect the kind of person you aspire to be—those who challenge you to grow closer to God, deepen your character, and pursue your purpose with integrity.

Think about the people who currently influence your life. Are they voices of encouragement, wisdom, and truth? Or are they pulling you in directions that distract from your calling? Choosing wisely doesn't mean cutting people off harshly, but it does mean being intentional about who you let speak into your life.

Even Jesus had an inner circle. Among the twelve disciples, Peter, James, and John were the ones He brought closest to Him in moments of prayer, transfiguration, and vulnerability. His example reminds us that not everyone has equal access to our hearts or minds, and that's okay; it doesn't mean you love them any less.

Your Board of Directors doesn't have to be large or formal. It could be a mentor who shares wisdom from their journey, a close friend who prays for you faithfully, or a family member who encourages you to stay grounded in your values. The key is to seek people who point you back to God and remind you of His promises.

Life was never meant to be navigated alone. When you surround yourself with wise counsel, you're not just building a support system—you're creating a community that strengthens your faith and sharpens your focus.

Plans fail for lack of counsel, but with many advisers they succeed.

— PROVERBS 15:22

LORD,

thank You for the gift of wise counsel and community. Help me to discern the voices I allow into my life and to seek guidance from those who reflect Your wisdom and truth. Surround me with people who encourage, challenge, and uplift me as I pursue the purpose You've placed in my heart. May I also be a source of wisdom and encouragement to others.

AMEN.

QUESTIONS TO CONSIDER:

1. Who are the people currently speaking into your life, and how are they influencing your decisions?
2. Are there voices you've been listening to that pull you away from God's purpose?
3. What qualities do you value most in a mentor or advisor?
4. How can you be more intentional about seeking wise and godly counsel in your daily life?
5. How does your current "council" align with the person God is calling you to become?

RIGHT NOW:

- Identify one person in your life who consistently offers wisdom, encouragement, or guidance. Write them a note of appreciation for their role in your journey.
- Reflect on your current circle of influence. Make a list of the voices in your life that align with your values and those that may be distracting you from your goals.

THIS WEEK:

- Reach out to a mentor, pastor, or trusted friend and ask for their perspective on a challenge or decision you're currently facing.
- Begin praying intentionally for God to bring the right people into your life to serve as wise counsel.

MOVING FORWARD:

- Build your Board of Directors. Choose three to five people who you can trust to speak truth into your life, challenge you when needed, and encourage you in your walk with God. Make time to regularly check in with these individuals.
- Evaluate your circle every few months, ensuring that the voices influencing you are helping you grow spiritually, emotionally, and purposefully.

Reminder:

You don't have to navigate life alone. Wise counsel builds clarity, strengthens faith, and keeps you aligned with God's purpose. Surround yourself with people who inspire you to grow and lift you higher.

Declutter Your Digital Life

The first step in crafting the life you want is to get rid of everything you don't.

— JOSHUA BECKER

Japanese organizational expert Marie Kondo discovered the life-changing magic of tidying up. Her approach wasn't just about having a clean house; it was about making room for joy by letting go of what no longer serves us. Her now-famous KonMari Method encourages people to ask a simple but powerful question about their possessions: "Does this spark joy?"

Today that same principle can be applied to our digital lives. In an age where emails pile up, phone notifications interrupt our peace, and social media demands our attention, digital clutter can overwhelm our minds just as much as physical clutter overwhelms our spaces, creating chaos that distracts us from what truly matters.

This principle connects with I Corinthians 14:40: "Everything should be done in a fitting and orderly way." God's nature is one of peace, not confusion. A cluttered digital environment often reflects and reinforces mental and spiritual chaos.

Studies from psychologists reveal that digital clutter—constant notifications, too many tabs open, or excessive screen time—increases stress, reduces productivity, and hinders focus. When we declutter our digital spaces, we create mental clarity and open ourselves to deeper connections with God, our purpose, and our community.

Think about your digital spaces right now. Are your inboxes overflowing with unread messages? Is your phone filled with apps you don't use? Are you constantly distracted by notifications that interrupt your quiet moments? Is there a social media platform that leaves you feeling empty when you log off? Just as clutter in our physical space can crowd out peace, digital clutter can crowd out the stillness we need to hear God's voice.

Even Jesus modeled intentional withdrawal from distractions. He often sought quiet places to reconnect with the Father. His example reminds us that creating intentional space—whether in our physical or digital lives—is essential for spiritual growth and peace.

Decluttering your digital life isn't just about deleting files or unfollowing accounts. It's an act of stewardship. By simplifying your digital environment, you create room for focus, intentionality, and connection. Those unused apps could be removed to give you a clearer home screen. That overwhelming inbox could be organized to free up mental energy. That social media platform can be replaced with a local social circle.

The process isn't just external; it's internal too. As you sort through your emails or social media accounts, you may find yourself reflecting on the habits, emotions, and patterns tied to them. It's an opportunity to invite God into the process, asking Him to reveal what is truly essential.

Remember, the goal isn't perfection. A perfectly organized inbox won't bring you closer to God, but a digital space that supports your faith and priorities will. By releasing what no longer serves you, you make room for the peace of Christ, the joy of His presence, and the clarity to pursue your calling with intention.

Everything should be done in a fitting and orderly way.

— I CORINTHIANS 14:40

LORD,
thank You for being a God of peace and order.
Help me to recognize the clutter in my life,
both physical and digital, that distracts me from You.
Guide me in creating space for stillness, focus,
and connection with You and others.
May my digital habits reflect my desire
to live intentionally and honor You in all I do.
AMEN.

QUESTIONS TO CONSIDER:

1. How does your current digital environment affect your mental and spiritual peace?
2. Are there specific apps, accounts, or notifications that consistently distract you from your priorities?
3. How often do you find yourself overwhelmed by unread emails, messages, or notifications?
4. What steps can you take to simplify your digital life and align it with God's purpose for you?
5. How can decluttering your digital spaces help you connect more deeply with God and others?

RIGHT NOW:

- Identify five apps, emails, or files you can delete immediately. Start with the easiest ones to let go of.
- Turn off unnecessary notifications on your phone or computer to reduce distractions.

THIS WEEK:

- Unsubscribe from email lists that no longer serve you or align with your goals.
- Create a folder system for your inbox to sort and archive emails, making it easier to manage.
- Dedicate thirty minutes to organizing your phone or computer, deleting unused apps and grouping similar ones together.

MOVING FORWARD:

- Establish a regular habit of digital decluttering, such as scheduling time each month to review and organize your inbox, files, and apps.
- Consider setting daily limits for screen time or taking one day each week to unplug and reconnect with God and loved ones.
- Be intentional about the digital content you consume, following accounts that inspire and align with your values while unfollowing those that drain your energy.

Reminder:

Simplifying your digital life creates space for clarity, peace, and the presence of God. Let go of what distracts you, and make room for what truly matters.

Capture Your Clarity

Paper has more patience than people.

— ANNE FRANK

Anne Frank's diary stands as one of the most poignant examples of how journaling can bring clarity, hope, and even a sense of peace in the midst of chaos. As a young Jewish girl hiding from the Nazis during World War II, Anne turned to her diary not only to document her experiences but also to process her emotions and find meaning in a world that seemed to have lost its way. Her simple yet profound reflection, "Paper has more patience than people," captures the essence of journaling: It's a space where thoughts can flow freely, without judgment, and where moments of clarity often emerge.

Anne's writing was not just an outlet for her fears and frustrations; it was also a place where she could dream, reflect, and reconnect with her sense of purpose. Despite the dire circumstances, her words reveal a deep awareness of life's beauty and God's presence. Her diary allowed her to document both her struggles and her hopes, creating a record of resilience that continues to inspire generations.

Psalm 77:11–12 says, "I will remember the deeds of the Lord; yes, I will remember Your miracles of long ago. I will consider all Your works and meditate on all Your mighty deeds." This Scripture invites us to reflect on God's faithfulness, even in challenging times. A breakthrough journal can serve a similar purpose, helping us capture the moments when God's presence feels clear and His promises come alive. When life becomes overwhelming, having a record of these moments reminds us of the clarity, vision, and promises He has given us.

Journaling goes deeper than recording the good times. It's about documenting the struggles, questions, and doubts too. These entries create a narrative of God's faithfulness, showing how He brings clarity and growth through both trials and triumphs. Anne's story reminds us that even in the darkest seasons, there are glimmers of hope and understanding waiting to be captured.

Psychologists have found that journaling reduces stress, improves mental health, and enhances problem-solving skills. Spiritually, it's a practice of intentional reflection, allowing us to process our thoughts and recognize God's hand in our lives. When we take the time to write down our moments of clarity, we create a resource we can return to when the path forward feels uncertain.

What would it look like for you to start a breakthrough journal? Perhaps it's as simple as jotting down a single insight each day: a verse that spoke to you, a prayer answered, or a moment when God's presence felt near. Over time, these reflections will become a map of His faithfulness.

Anne Frank's diary reminds us of the power of writing to make sense of the world and reconnect with our faith. As you document your own journey, may you find clarity, hope, and a deeper trust in God's promises. Your breakthrough journal might just become a testament to His ongoing work in your life.

I will remember the deeds of the LORD; yes, I will remember Your miracles of long ago. I will consider all Your works and meditate on all Your mighty deeds.

— PSALM 77:11-12

LORD,

thank You for being with me in every moment of my journey. Help me to reflect on Your faithfulness, both in times of joy and in seasons of struggle. Give me the clarity to see Your hand in my life and the wisdom to document the moments where Your promises shine brightest. May my words honor You and remind me of Your never-failing love.

AMEN.

QUESTIONS TO CONSIDER:

1. When was the last time you felt God's presence clearly in your life?
2. How has journaling—or reflecting on past experiences—helped you process challenges or find clarity?
3. What patterns or themes have you noticed when looking back on God's faithfulness in your life?
4. Are there moments of doubt or struggle you feel called to process through writing?
5. How might a record of your journey help you navigate future uncertainties?

RIGHT NOW:

- Start by writing down one recent moment when you felt God's presence or clarity. Describe the emotions, thoughts, or circumstances surrounding it.
- Choose a notebook, journal, or digital platform to dedicate as your "breakthrough journal."

THIS WEEK:

- Reflect on three moments from your past when God brought you through a challenge or fulfilled a promise. Write about what you learned in those situations.
- Include one Scripture, prayer, or quote that has inspired you recently.
- Set aside ten minutes each day for intentional journaling. Use this time to capture thoughts, prayers, or experiences that stand out.

MOVING FORWARD:

- Build a habit of journaling consistently, whether it's daily, weekly, or at significant moments.
- Look back through your entries at the end of each month and note any recurring themes or areas where God's guidance was evident.
- Share parts of your breakthrough journal with a trusted friend or mentor as a way to reflect and celebrate God's faithfulness together.

Reminder:

Journaling isn't just about capturing words; it's about creating a record of God's faithfulness and discovering His presence in every chapter of your story.

Theme Your Days

The key is not to prioritize what's on your schedule, but to schedule your priorities.

— STEPHEN COVEY

Genesis 1 gives us a profound example of focus and intentionality. In the creation story, God didn't create the entire universe in one sweeping moment. Instead, He assigned specific tasks to each day: light on one day, the separation of land and sea on another, and the creation of living creatures on another. By the end of the sixth day, the work was complete, and on the seventh, God rested. This pattern of intentional focus reminds us of the power of assigning specific goals to specific times.

God's act of creation shows us that even the most monumental tasks can be broken into manageable pieces when approached with purpose and clarity. This approach is particularly relevant for artists, such as writers, who balance the complexities of brainstorming, researching, writing, and editing their work. What if we took a page from God's book and structured our creative processes with the same intentionality?

Genesis 1:31 says, "God saw all that He had made, and it was very good. And there was evening, and there was morning—the sixth day." By the end of each day, God looked back and saw that His work was good. This practice of assigning tasks to specific days and then reflecting on them is a model we can follow in our own lives. For a writer, "Theme Days" could mean dedicating Mondays to brainstorming and gathering inspiration, Tuesdays to researching, Wednesdays to drafting, and Thursdays to refining details.

Imagine how this structure could bring clarity and flow to your creative process. Instead of feeling overwhelmed by the enormity of a mural project, breaking it into focused days allows you to fully engage with each stage of the work. It also gives space for reflection, where you can pause and appreciate your progress, just as God reflected on His creation and declared it good.

Research supports this idea, stating that focusing on one task at a time—a practice known as "monotasking"—increases efficiency and reduces mental fatigue. Spiritually, this practice mirrors God's example of deliberate and focused action, reminding us that we were not created to live in constant chaos.

Creating Theme Days isn't just about getting things done; it's about honoring the rhythm of work and rest that God designed for us. By assigning specific focus areas to each day, we can approach our responsibilities with intention, knowing that there is a time and season for everything (Ecclesiastes 3:1). By creating structure, you're not only organizing your time but also aligning it with God's example of intentionality and purpose.

The creation story teaches us that there is beauty in order and clarity in focus. When we align our daily lives with this principle, we create space for meaningful work, intentional rest, and a deeper connection with God's design for our lives. So, take a step back, plan your Theme Days, and trust that God will guide your efforts to completion.

God saw all that He had made, and it was very good. And there was evening, and there was morning—the sixth day.

— GENESIS 1:31

LORD,

thank You for the example You set through creation—working with focus, reflecting on progress, and honoring rest. Help me to bring structure and purpose to my days, aligning my tasks with Your rhythm of intentionality. May my work be meaningful and my rest be restorative, so I can fully glorify You in all that I do.

AMEN.

QUESTIONS TO CONSIDER:

1. What areas of your life feel chaotic or overwhelming right now?
2. How might breaking tasks into specific focus days bring clarity and peace to your schedule?
3. What part of your current routine could benefit from more structure and intentionality?
4. How do you currently reflect on your work, and how can you create moments to pause and appreciate progress?
5. Are there areas in your schedule where you need to honor rest, as God did on the seventh day?

RIGHT NOW:

- Write down the top three tasks or projects that are currently consuming your attention. For each one, identify the specific steps required to complete it.
- Choose one task and assign a day this week to focus on just that step.

THIS WEEK:

- Create a daily or weekly schedule with themes for specific tasks or responsibilities (e.g., planning, execution, reflection, rest).
- Dedicate one day to reflection. At the end of that day, write down what went well, what could improve, and where you saw God's hand in your efforts.
- Intentionally schedule one day or a block of time for rest to recharge and refocus.

MOVING FORWARD:

- Build a rhythm that includes both work and rest, aligning with God's design for balance and intentionality.
- Regularly evaluate your "Theme Days" and adjust as needed to stay aligned with your goals and priorities.
- Make space in your schedule for reflection at the end of each day or week, celebrating the progress you've made and offering any challenges to God in prayer.

Reminder:

There is beauty in structure and power in focus. When you align your days with purpose, you create space for God to work through you.

Map Your Impact

Act as if what you do makes a difference. It does.

— WILLIAM JAMES

Wangari Maathai, the late Kenyan environmentalist and Nobel Peace Prize winner, understood the power of one action to ripple outward and create lasting change. She founded the Green Belt Movement, an environmental organization that has led to the planting of millions of trees across Africa. What began as a grassroots initiative to combat deforestation and empower women grew into a global movement. Maathai's legacy is a testament to the profound impact one person can have when they follow their purpose and make intentional decisions.

Her journey teaches us an important principle: Every action we take, no matter how small it seems, has the potential to create a ripple effect far beyond what we can see. Maathai famously said, "It's the little things citizens do. That's what will make the difference. My little thing is planting trees."

Jesus calls us to be the salt of the earth and the light of the world (Matthew 5:13–16). He encourages us to let our light shine before others so that they may see our good works and glorify our Father in heaven. Our decisions and our influence matter. They have the power to impact those around us, and that impact can radiate outward, affecting entire communities, nations, and even the world.

Impact mapping is the practice of tracking how your actions, no matter how small, affect those around you. It's about being intentional with your choices, understanding the consequences of your actions, and recognizing the ripple effects they create. Just as Wangari Maathai's actions led to a movement, your daily decisions—whether they seem large or small—can make a significant difference in the lives of others.

By mapping the impact of your actions, you can begin to see the ways in which your purpose aligns with the needs of the world. You can identify patterns and uncover areas where you can be more intentional in creating positive change. Impact mapping invites you to look beyond yourself and consider how your decisions and actions can serve others, honor God, and advance His Kingdom.

Wangari Maathai's impact didn't happen overnight, and it wasn't without challenges. But she remained steadfast, driven by a vision for a better world. Her work reminds us that our small acts, when multiplied over time and through the power of community, can lead to significant transformation. Every tree planted, every person empowered, every life touched—these are the ripples of impact that continue to reverberate today.

As you reflect on the choices you make, take the time to map out the impact of your actions. Ask yourself: *How does what I do affect others? How can my choices today bring light and hope to the world around me?* Use this practice to make intentional decisions that honor God's calling on your life and leave a lasting legacy of positive change.

Let your light shine in ways that touch lives and build a better world, just as Wangari Maathai's light continues to shine through the Green Belt Movement and her lifelong dedication to the planet and its people.

You are the light of the world. A town built on a hill cannot be hidden. Neither do people light a lamp and put it under a bowl. Instead, they put it on its stand, and it gives light to everyone in the house. In the same way, let your light shine before others, that they may see your good deeds and glorify your Father in heaven.

— MATTHEW 5:13–16

LORD,

thank You for calling me to be a light in the world and for giving me the power to create change through my actions. Help me to see the ripple effects of my choices, and guide me to be intentional in the ways I serve You and others. May my actions glorify You and bring hope, light, and transformation to those around me.

AMEN.

QUESTIONS TO CONSIDER:

1. What actions, big or small, have had a positive ripple effect on others in your life?
2. How can you align your daily choices with God's purpose for you?
3. Are there areas in your life where you've underestimated the impact of your actions?
4. How can you be more intentional about serving others in your community?
5. What is one way you can use your unique gifts to honor God and leave a lasting legacy?

RIGHT NOW:

- Reflect on one recent action you've taken that had a positive effect on someone else. Consider how it might have impacted them.
- Think of one small, intentional action you can take today to bring light to someone's life.

THIS WEEK:

- Identify an area in your life where you can make intentional choices to serve others.
- Begin an Impact Map Journal. Each evening, jot down one action you took and the potential ripple effects it created.
- Seek out a group where you can amplify your efforts.

MOVING FORWARD:

- Set a long-term goal that aligns your actions with God's purpose.
- Revisit your Impact Map Journal regularly to reflect on how your actions are creating ripples of change and how you can continue to grow in intentionality.
- Pray for guidance in maximizing your influence for God's glory and the good of others.

Reminder:

Every small action has the potential to create ripples of hope and transformation. Let your light shine boldly, trusting God to use your efforts for His greater purpose.

"I find joy in
showing grace
to myself and
others."

INTERVIEW 4:

Rediscovering Purpose After Health Scares

BY: SUSAN KUENZI
RETIRED COUNSELOR | WRITER

1: What are you reigniting, reawakening, rediscovering, or reclaiming in this season?

A: I went through a challenging time during the pandemic. Living with multiple sclerosis, I experienced falls and concussions, and my husband faced health issues. We also dealt with major family losses, leaving me overwhelmed and in a crisis of meaning. I stopped writing and helping others, feeling isolated and lost. Over the past couple of years, God has reignited my sense of purpose and calling as a writer and vessel of His love.

A turning point came when my college roommate called me from Japan. She shared her decision to enjoy life at sixty, inspiring me to embrace life at my best—despite pain or circumstances. That decision restored my joy and peace. My husband and I moved to a healthier environment, and I adopted a service dog for mobility. We built a backyard writer's cabin, and I reopened my coaching business, Tenderly Transformed. I'm also writing a book, *Tenderly Transformed: Growing and Healing Through Turbulent Times*, which brings me so much joy.

2: What challenges have you faced in this process, and what have they taught you?

A: Living with MS creates daily challenges like fatigue and mobility issues, compounded by a torn retina after surgery last year. I often need help with physical tasks, but I pray that my needs become blessings for others, not burdens. God has always provided through my husband, friends, and His love.

During a dark season, I felt distant from God and struggled with shame and depression. Yet He restored my sense of security in Him. These experiences gave me deep compassion for others and a stronger understanding of God's steadfast love.

3: What unexpected joys or revelations have come from this process?

A: I've found joy in seeing God touch lives through my struggles. Writing and helping others now carry a renewed sense of calling and purpose. God's love and presence continually strengthen me.

4: Has this journey reshaped the way you define success or fulfillment?

A: Success is no longer tied to achievements but to helping others heal and grow in God. I find joy in showing grace to myself and others.

5: What advice would you give someone who feels stuck in a similar rut?

A: Be honest about your struggles, and lean into God's love. Seek professional help if needed, and remember—God can redeem the hardest times for good.

Make a Promise

Dear past, thank you for your lessons. Dear future, I'm ready.

— UNKNOWN

In 2010 MTV launched a show called *When I Was 17*, where celebrities reflected on the triumphs, mistakes, and lessons they learned as teenagers. The show was a nostalgic glimpse into the younger selves of people who had achieved great things, offering insight into how their youthful dreams and struggles shaped their futures. Watching these stories unfold, one can't help but wonder: What would these individuals have said to their future selves at that age? What advice, hopes, or dreams would they have captured in a letter?

Barack Obama's journey offers a real-life example of this practice. As a young man navigating identity, purpose, and ambition, Obama often wrote letters to himself. In his memoir *Dreams from My Father*, he reflects on his early struggles to make sense of his heritage and find his place in the world. These moments of introspection and writing became a way for him to clarify his goals and remind himself of the vision he held for his life. These letters were not just about capturing thoughts but also about aligning his actions with the future he envisioned.

Writing a letter to your future self is a powerful act of faith and intentionality. Jeremiah 29:11 reminds us of God's promise: "'For I know the plans I have for you,' declares the LORD, 'plans to prosper you and not to harm you, plans to give you hope and a future.'" Putting pen to paper allows you to articulate your hopes, dreams, and the promises you're making to yourself and to God. It's a tangible way to remind yourself of the clarity and vision you have in the present, so that during times of doubt or difficulty, you can return to those words and be encouraged.

Studies in psychology reveal that imagining and writing to your future self increases motivation and accountability. When you write down your aspirations and envision the person you want to become, you create a connection between your present and future selves. Spiritually, this practice aligns with the biblical call to reflect on God's faithfulness and anticipate His work in your life.

Imagine sitting down to write a letter that your future self will read in one, five, or ten years. What would you want to remind yourself of? Perhaps it's the strength you showed during a challenging season, the promises God has spoken over your life, or the dreams you're working toward. Maybe you'd write about the values you hope to uphold or the relationships you want to nurture. These reflections create a snapshot of your faith, character, and vision.

When I Was 17 reminds us that everyone starts somewhere. Barack Obama's letters to himself show how introspection can guide us toward our purpose. Your letter doesn't have to be perfect; it just has to be honest. Take a moment to write to your future self. Share your hopes, your dreams, and the promises you're making today. As you do, invite God into the process, trusting that He will guide your steps and fulfill His plans for your life. One day, when you revisit your letter, you may be amazed at how far you've come and how faithful God has been along the way.

“For I know the plans I have for you,” declares the Lord, “plans to prosper you and not to harm you, plans to give you hope and a future.”

— JEREMIAH 29:11

LORD,
thank You for the gift of hope and the future You have planned for me. Help me to align my dreams and aspirations with Your purpose. As I reflect on the promises I am making today, give me the courage to follow through and the faith to trust Your guidance.
AMEN.

QUESTIONS TO CONSIDER:

1. If you could write one message to your future self, what would it say about the season you're currently in?
2. What promises has God placed on your heart for your life and your purpose?
3. How have past challenges shaped the vision you have for your future?
4. What do you want your future self to remember about God's faithfulness in this season?
5. How can you ensure your current actions align with the person you want to become?

RIGHT NOW:

- Take fifteen minutes to write a letter to your future self. Include your hopes, dreams, and promises, as well as encouragement for the challenges you may face. Seal it and set a date to open it in the future.
- Reflect on Jeremiah 29:11, and write down the ways you've seen God's plans for hope and a future at work in your life.

THIS WEEK:

- Identify one specific promise you've made to yourself or God and take the first step toward fulfilling it. This could be starting a habit, taking action on a goal, or deepening a relationship.
- Create a space—whether a journal, a folder, or a digital file—where you can store letters or reflections for your future self. Use it to track your growth and God's faithfulness over time.

MOVING FORWARD:

- Set a recurring date to revisit your letter and reflect on the progress you've made. Celebrate milestones and realign your actions with your vision.
- Begin praying over your future self and the dreams God has placed on your heart, asking for His guidance, protection, and provision as you walk toward His plans.

Reminder:

You are writing a legacy of faith and purpose with every decision you make. Trust that God's plans for you are greater than you can imagine, and let your words today serve as a reminder of His promises tomorrow.

List Your Limits

Success is not the absence of failure;
it's the persistence through failure.

— AISHA TYLER

In 1962 author and entrepreneur Jim Rohn shared a simple yet profound idea: "You are the average of the five people you spend the most time with." What if this idea expanded beyond just people to include habits, activities, and mindsets? What if we are also the sum of what we choose to engage in? The things that drain our energy and keep us stuck often go unnoticed, but they can subtly shape our lives, prevent our growth, and keep us from fully stepping into the plans God has for us.

Hebrews 12:1 (NKJV) encourages us to "lay aside every weight, and the sin which so easily ensnares us." This passage highlights how some things—while not necessarily sinful—can still slow us down. There are activities, mindsets, and even relationships that drain us emotionally, spiritually, and physically. These "weights" can be habits, tasks, or situations that no longer serve our purpose or God's calling on our lives. Just like an athlete shedding excess weight to run a race, we, too, must let go of what hinders us.

In 2018 a study published by the American Psychological Association found that people who identify and eliminate distractions tend to perform at higher levels. Similarly, in our spiritual and personal lives, when we consciously "stop doing" certain things, we free up mental space, time, and energy for what truly matters. This is what Hebrews 12:1

is calling us to do—focus on the race set before us and leave behind distractions that hold us back.

The key to a more fulfilling and intentional life lies in recognizing what is no longer serving us. Whether it's time spent scrolling social media, constantly overcommitting to others, or dwelling on past mistakes, these things add weight to our journey. This is where a "Stop Doing" List comes into play.

Creating a "Stop Doing" List helps you eliminate what's depleting your energy or distracting you from your mission. By identifying activities that drain you, you make room for actions that energize and empower you. For example, if you find yourself overwhelmed by unnecessary commitments, it might be time to say no to a few things. If you feel mentally fatigued after certain conversations or environments, it could be time to limit exposure to those situations.

Sometimes the hardest part is recognizing what to stop. We might resist letting go of things out of habit or fear of disappointing others. But remember that by eliminating these distractions, you are giving yourself the gift of focus and clarity. Just as Jesus often withdrew to quiet places to pray (Luke 5:16), we, too, need space to rest and refocus.

Take a moment today to write your own "Stop Doing" List. Look at the areas in your life where you feel weighed down, and ask God for the wisdom to know what needs to go. Trust that by removing the unnecessary, you make room for God's peace, joy, and purpose to fill you up. You're not just making space in your schedule—you're making space for your soul to thrive.

Therefore, since we are surrounded by such a great cloud of witnesses, let us throw off everything that hinders and the sin that so easily entangles. And let us run with perseverance the race marked out for us.

— HEBREWS 12:1

LORD,

help me to identify the things in my life that are holding me back from fully living out Your purpose. Give me the courage to release what no longer serves me and to trust in Your plan. Fill the space I create with Your peace, joy, and guidance.

AMEN.

QUESTIONS TO CONSIDER:

1. What habits, activities, or relationships feel draining instead of life-giving?
2. Are there any commitments or obligations you've taken on out of guilt rather than purpose?
3. How do you feel after spending time in certain environments or with specific people?
4. What weights—emotional, mental, or physical—are slowing you down in your spiritual journey?
5. How can releasing certain distractions help you focus more on God's calling for your life?

RIGHT NOW:

- Write your "Stop Doing" List. Take a blank sheet of paper and list the habits, tasks, or commitments that feel burdensome or misaligned with your purpose.
- Identify one thing from your list you can stop immediately and take action on it today.

THIS WEEK:

- Begin saying no to commitments or requests that add unnecessary weight to your life. Start small—choose one area where you often overcommit and set boundaries.
- Spend ten minutes each evening reflecting on your day. Ask yourself: *What could I have avoided or done differently to feel more aligned with God's peace and purpose?*

MOVING FORWARD:

- Regularly review and update your "Stop Doing" List. As new distractions arise, evaluate whether they're adding value or hindering your growth.
- Make a habit of intentionally scheduling rest and quiet time with God, as Jesus did, to ensure you have the clarity and energy to focus on your mission.

Reminder:
Letting go isn't about losing—it's about making space for God to work in you and through you.

Date New Ideas

Creativity doesn't wait for that perfect moment.
It fashions its own perfect moments out of ordinary ones.
— BRUCE GARRABRANDT

Donald Glover is a modern Renaissance man. From his early days writing for *30 Rock* to his Emmy-winning work on *Atlanta*, his Grammy-winning music as Childish Gambino, and even his forays into acting in films like *Solo: A Star Wars Story*, Glover exemplifies the art of exploration. He has never confined himself to a single identity, title, or medium. Instead, he constantly reinvents himself, pursuing new creative outlets with curiosity and boldness.

In interviews, Glover has spoken about how his diverse pursuits feed into one another. His work as a writer informs his music; his experiences as an actor shape his directing. By exploring multiple disciplines, he's created a career that defies categorization, proving that innovation often comes from being open to new ideas and perspectives. Glover's willingness to embrace the unfamiliar has made him one of the most dynamic creators of our time.

This spirit of curiosity aligns with I John 4:1, which says, "Test the spirits to see whether they are from God." This verse reminds us to engage with new opportunities and ideas, not recklessly, but with discernment and an open heart. "Idea dating" is about trying new creative ventures—not to commit to all of them but to discover what resonates with your soul and aligns with God's unique purpose for you.

Taking the time to "date" new ideas doesn't require an immediate commitment. It's about embracing curiosity and the willingness to step into unfamiliar territory. Whether it's launching a pop-up business, selling your photography online, or auditioning for a local stage production, let your creativity flow freely without judgment. You may find that some ideas won't be for you, while others will blossom into something deeply meaningful. The act of exploring itself, however, is where the transformation happens.

Research in creativity reveals that exploring diverse interests can boost problem-solving skills and foster innovation. When you step outside of your comfort zone, you expose yourself to new ways of thinking and unlock parts of yourself that may have been dormant. This practice invites God into your journey, asking Him to reveal what fits into His plan for your life.

Donald Glover's story teaches us that you don't have to have everything figured out before you start. Trying something new doesn't mean abandoning who you are; it means adding new layers to your identity. Each new interest you explore can teach you something about yourself and the world around you.

As you embark on your journey of "idea dating," remember that God delights in your exploration. He created you with unique talents, interests, and curiosities for a reason. By testing the waters and stepping into the unknown, you're not only discovering more about yourself but also uncovering the depths of God's creativity within you. So go ahead: Try something new, and let the adventure begin.

Dear friends, do not believe every spirit, but test the spirits to see whether they are from God, because many false prophets have gone out into the world.

— I JOHN 4:1

LORD,

thank You for the creativity You've placed within me. Help me to explore new ideas with discernment and courage, trusting that You will guide me toward the ones that align with Your plan for my life. Open my heart to possibilities, and let my exploration be a reflection of Your endless creativity.

AMEN.

QUESTIONS TO CONSIDER:

1. What creative ideas or hobbies have been on your heart but you've hesitated to try?
2. Are there areas in your life where you've felt stagnant and in need of fresh inspiration?
3. How can trying something new deepen your connection with God and His purpose for you?
4. When you consider new ideas, do you approach them with excitement, fear, or a mix of both? Why?
5. How can embracing curiosity enhance your personal, professional, or spiritual growth?

RIGHT NOW:

- Make a list of three creative or new activities you've always wanted to try but haven't yet. Examples could include taking a dance class, writing poetry, or experimenting with photography.
- Choose one item from your list and commit to exploring it this week. Take the first step, whether that's researching, signing up, or starting right away.

THIS WEEK:

- Spend fifteen to thirty minutes each day trying something new. This doesn't have to be a major project—small experiments like cooking a new recipe or doodling in a notebook can spark creativity.
- Reflect on how the new activity makes you feel. Does it energize you? Challenge you? Reveal something about yourself?

MOVING FORWARD:

- Make "idea dating" a regular practice. Schedule monthly or biweekly sessions where you intentionally try something new. This could include visiting a library, listening to a new podcast, or attending a workshop.
- Start journaling your experiences. Write about what you've learned, what excites you, and how each new idea is shaping your perspective.

Reminder:

Exploration isn't about perfect results—it's about discovering the creativity God has already placed within you. Trust the journey and enjoy the process!

Set Your Standards

It is our choices that show what we truly are, far more than our abilities.

— J.K. ROWLING

In 1978 Warren Buffett, one of the world's most successful investors, sat down to share advice with a group of young professionals. He asked them to list the twenty-five goals they wanted to accomplish. Once they'd written them down, he instructed them to circle the top five, the ones that truly mattered most. Then he gave this simple but profound advice: "Now, you've got two lists. Focus all your energy on the five you circled. For the other twenty, avoid them at all costs."

Buffett's strategy highlights the importance of decision filters—criteria to help us say yes to what truly aligns with our values and no to the distractions that can lead us off course. Every day, we face hundreds of choices, and if we don't have a clear framework to guide us, we risk spreading ourselves too thin and losing focus on our highest priorities.

James 1:5 (NKJV) encourages us to ask God for wisdom: "If any of you lacks wisdom, let him ask of God, who gives to all liberally and without reproach, and it will be given to him." God is always ready to provide the wisdom we need to make the right choices. When we develop decision filters, we create a structure that helps us discern what is best, not just what is easiest or most urgent.

Modern psychology tells us that humans are naturally inclined to avoid cognitive overload. When we make decisions without clear criteria, we increase our mental and emotional strain. Decision fatigue sets in, making it harder to prioritize, and we may end up saying yes to things that aren't in alignment with our true goals.

Creating decision filters can simplify this process. By outlining a set of criteria—such as alignment with your core values, long-term impact, or the ability to contribute to your personal or professional growth—you can quickly evaluate opportunities and commitments. Over time, this approach helps reduce the mental clutter and provides clarity about where to invest your energy.

Steve Jobs, the cofounder of Apple, famously used this principle. He would often say no to good ideas so that he could say yes to great ones. He believed that focusing on fewer projects and giving them his undivided attention was the key to success. His disciplined approach to decision-making allowed him to stay aligned with his larger vision and avoid the distractions that could easily derail his focus.

One of the greatest gifts we can give ourselves is the ability to say no with confidence. Our yes should be reserved for the things that truly matter, the things that align with the calling and vision God has placed in our hearts.

Psalm 119:105 (NKJV) reminds us, "Your word is a lamp to my feet and a light to my path." When we allow God's word to guide our decisions, we can rest assured that He will lead us to the right choices, the ones that will bring us peace and fulfillment.

By building decision filters that are rooted in wisdom and clarity, we can navigate the complexity of life with confidence and purpose, trusting that our decisions today are setting the stage for a bright and meaningful future.

If any of you lacks wisdom, let him ask of God, who gives to all liberally and without reproach, and it will be given to him.

— JAMES 1:5

HEAVENLY FATHER,

thank You for Your gift of wisdom and discernment. Help me create standards that align with Your purpose for my life. Guide my decisions so that I may focus on what matters most and let go of distractions that pull me away from Your plan. Teach me to trust in Your wisdom and follow the path You've laid out for me.

AMEN.

QUESTIONS TO CONSIDER:

1. What are the top five values or goals that guide your life right now?
2. How often do you say yes to commitments that don't align with your long-term purpose?
3. What distractions have been pulling you away from what matters most?
4. How can God's wisdom help you establish clearer boundaries in your decision-making?
5. What would it look like to confidently say no to good opportunities in favor of great ones?

RIGHT NOW:

- Write down your top five core values or priorities that reflect what truly matters in your life. These could include faith, family, personal growth, health, or professional goals.
- Create a simple decision filter based on these values. For example, ask yourself: *Does this align with my long-term goals? Does it bring me closer to God's calling for my life?*

THIS WEEK:

- Evaluate your current commitments. Make a list of the activities, projects, or relationships that consume your time and energy. Highlight the ones that align with your core values and circle the ones that don't.
- Begin to let go of one thing this week that isn't serving your priorities or God's purpose for your life.

MOVING FORWARD:

- Practice saying no with grace and confidence. When new opportunities arise, refer to your decision filter to determine if they align with your priorities.
- Schedule regular check-ins—perhaps monthly or quarterly—to review your commitments and ensure they continue to align with your values and goals.

Reminder:

Your yes is powerful—reserve it for the things that matter most. When you set your standards, you create space for God's best in your life.

Debrief Your Week

The more I know, the more I realize how much I don't know.

— MAYA ANGELOU

In the early 1990s, Dr. Maya Angelou, renowned poet, author, and civil rights activist, was invited to give a speech to a group of young leaders. During her talk, she shared her philosophy on learning, emphasizing the importance of reflection and self-awareness. "When you know better, you do better," she famously said, underlining that growth doesn't come from simply experiencing life—it comes from learning and adjusting based on those experiences.

This approach aligns closely with the biblical invitation in Psalm 139:23–24: "Search me, O God, and know my heart; test me and know my anxious thoughts. See if there is any offensive way in me, and lead me in the way everlasting." Reflection is not just a passive process; it's an active step toward spiritual and personal growth, where you invite God to examine your life, reveal lessons, and guide you toward greater wisdom.

Maya Angelou's work exemplified this commitment to personal reflection. She understood the power of learning from both triumphs and failures. Her works, including *I Know Why the Caged Bird Sings* and *Letter to My Daughter*, offer insights into her reflective process, often revisiting pivotal moments from her past to extract wisdom and inspiration. Angelou didn't shy away from reflecting on her mistakes; she embraced them as opportunities for growth, which ultimately shaped her powerful voice.

In the business world, companies like Google have incorporated regular "debate sessions" where teams analyze both successes and failures to understand what worked and what didn't. These sessions are key to improving performance and fostering a culture of continuous learning. Google's approach is rooted in the belief that learning from both outcomes is crucial for progress.

Similarly, you can apply the principle of weekly debriefs to your life. Each week, set aside time for personal reflection. Think about the victories, the struggles, and the lessons learned in your professional, personal, and spiritual journeys. What decisions did you make that were aligned with your values? What actions need revising? Just as Maya Angelou continuously grew by reflecting on her experiences, you, too, can refine your life's direction through regular review.

The benefits of weekly debriefs extend beyond personal growth. They enhance your ability to be more present, make better decisions, and deepen your relationship with God. By inviting God into this process of reflection, you allow Him to guide you into a more purposeful, joyful life. You also gain clarity in areas where you may have been stuck, and you set yourself on a path toward greater alignment with your true calling.

As you make weekly debriefs a habit, focus on the lessons God wants to teach you. These debriefs become spiritual practice, helping you stay grounded in His truth and ensuring you walk in His wisdom with each passing week.

Search me, O God, and know my heart; test me and know my anxious thoughts. See if there is any offensive way in me, and lead me in the way everlasting.

— PSALM 139:23–24

FATHER,

thank You for being with me through every triumph and challenge this week. Search my heart and reveal the lessons I need to learn. Guide me as I reflect on my experiences, align my actions with Your will, and lead me closer to the life You have called me to live.

AMEN.

QUESTIONS TO CONSIDER:

1. What victories did you experience this week, and how did they align with your values and purpose?
2. What challenges did you face, and how might God be using them to teach you something important?
3. Did any decisions or actions leave you feeling out of alignment with God's calling?
4. How did you experience God's presence this week, and what moments brought you closer to Him?
5. What specific area in your life could benefit from more intentional focus or adjustment next week?

RIGHT NOW:

- Take ten minutes to journal about one key moment from your week—whether it was a success, a failure, or a moment of clarity. Reflect on what you learned and how it impacted your heart or mindset.

THIS WEEK:

- Schedule thirty minutes at the end of the week to review your week intentionally. Break your reflections into three parts:
    1. **Wins:** What went well, and what are you thankful for?
    2. **Lessons:** What didn't go as planned, and what can you learn from it?
    3. **Adjustments:** What habits, thoughts, or actions will you carry forward or revise next week?

MOVING FORWARD:

- Establish a weekly debrief habit. Choose a consistent day and time—perhaps Sunday evening or Friday afternoon—to reflect on your week and invite God to guide your thoughts and plans for the future.
- Share one takeaway from your weekly debrief with a trusted friend, mentor, or accountability partner for encouragement and feedback.

Reminder:

Every week is an opportunity to learn, grow, and align more closely with God's purpose for your life. Reflect, adjust, and move forward in faith.

Count Your Skills

The greatest deception men suffer is from their own opinions.

— LEONARDO DA VINCI

In his early twenties, Leonardo da Vinci was a master of many fields—art, science, engineering, anatomy, and more. His notebooks, filled with sketches and writings, reveal a man driven by curiosity and an unyielding desire to understand the world around him. Da Vinci's skillset went far beyond just painting; he was a true Renaissance man who combined various talents and knowledge into his masterpieces, from the *Mona Lisa* to groundbreaking anatomical drawings.

One of the most powerful aspects of da Vinci's genius was his ability to integrate multiple disciplines into a cohesive whole. His artistic skills were deeply informed by his understanding of the human body, physics, and geometry. For example, his study of human anatomy enabled him to paint realistic human figures with unprecedented accuracy, while his engineering knowledge gave him the ability to design complex mechanical devices. His skills inventory wasn't confined to any one category—it spanned a vast array of interests and fields, allowing him to create innovative, transformative works that changed the course of history.

The same principle can apply to you. Sometimes we get so focused on one area of our lives—especially our careers—that we forget about the other skills and gifts we possess. First Peter 4:10 reminds us that "each of you should use *whatever* gift you have received to serve others, as faithful stewards of God's grace in its various forms" (emphasis added). It's not just about what you do in your job but how your other abilities can serve and impact others.

Your personal skills inventory is more than a list of professional qualifications; it's a holistic view of everything you bring to the table. Think about the hobbies you enjoy—whether it's cooking, photography, or playing an instrument. Consider the emotional intelligence you bring to relationships, your ability to connect with people, and your leadership qualities. These abilities, even if not part of your professional identity, are just as important in fulfilling your purpose.

By recognizing and nurturing all your gifts—both the ones you're paid for and the ones God gave you—you become more effective and balanced in all aspects of your life. Much like da Vinci, you have the potential to merge different areas of expertise to create something extraordinary. Your skills inventory doesn't just reflect what you can do—it reflects who you are and the diverse ways God has equipped you to impact the world around you.

As you begin to identify and acknowledge all the talents and gifts that make up your unique skillset, you'll gain a fuller understanding of your God-given potential. This awareness opens the door to creative ways to serve others, use your strengths in new contexts, and grow as a person who brings value in every area of life.

Each of you should use whatever gift you have received to serve others, as faithful stewards of God's grace in its various forms.

— I PETER 4:10

LORD,

thank You for the unique gifts and abilities You have placed within me. Help me to recognize and steward them well, not only for my growth but for Your glory. Teach me how to use my skills to serve others and fulfill the purpose You've designed for me.

AMEN.

QUESTIONS TO CONSIDER:

1. What are three skills or talents you naturally excel at, even if you don't often acknowledge them?
2. How have your unique skills made a difference in the lives of others?
3. What hobbies or interests bring you joy, and how might they be connected to your broader purpose?
4. Are there any overlooked abilities or gifts you haven't fully explored or developed?
5. How can you combine multiple skills to create something meaningful and impactful?

RIGHT NOW:

- Write down ten skills or talents you currently have, no matter how small or unrelated they may seem. Think beyond professional abilities to include personal strengths like empathy, adaptability, or creativity.

THIS WEEK:

- Reflect on how you've used one of your skills to help someone else recently. Was it through your job, a hobby, or an act of kindness? Journal about the experience and how it made you feel.
- Explore one underutilized skill by dedicating an hour to practice, learn, or use it in a new way.

MOVING FORWARD:

- Create a "skills inventory" by listing all your talents, hobbies, and areas of expertise. Highlight the ones you feel align most closely with God's purpose for your life.
- Identify two or three ways you can use your skills to serve others, whether it's volunteering, mentoring, or creating something new that meets a need.
- Pray regularly for God to reveal opportunities where your unique abilities can make a difference in His Kingdom.

Reminder:

You are a masterpiece crafted by God, equipped with unique skills and talents designed to impact the world in ways only you can. Celebrate your gifts and steward them faithfully!

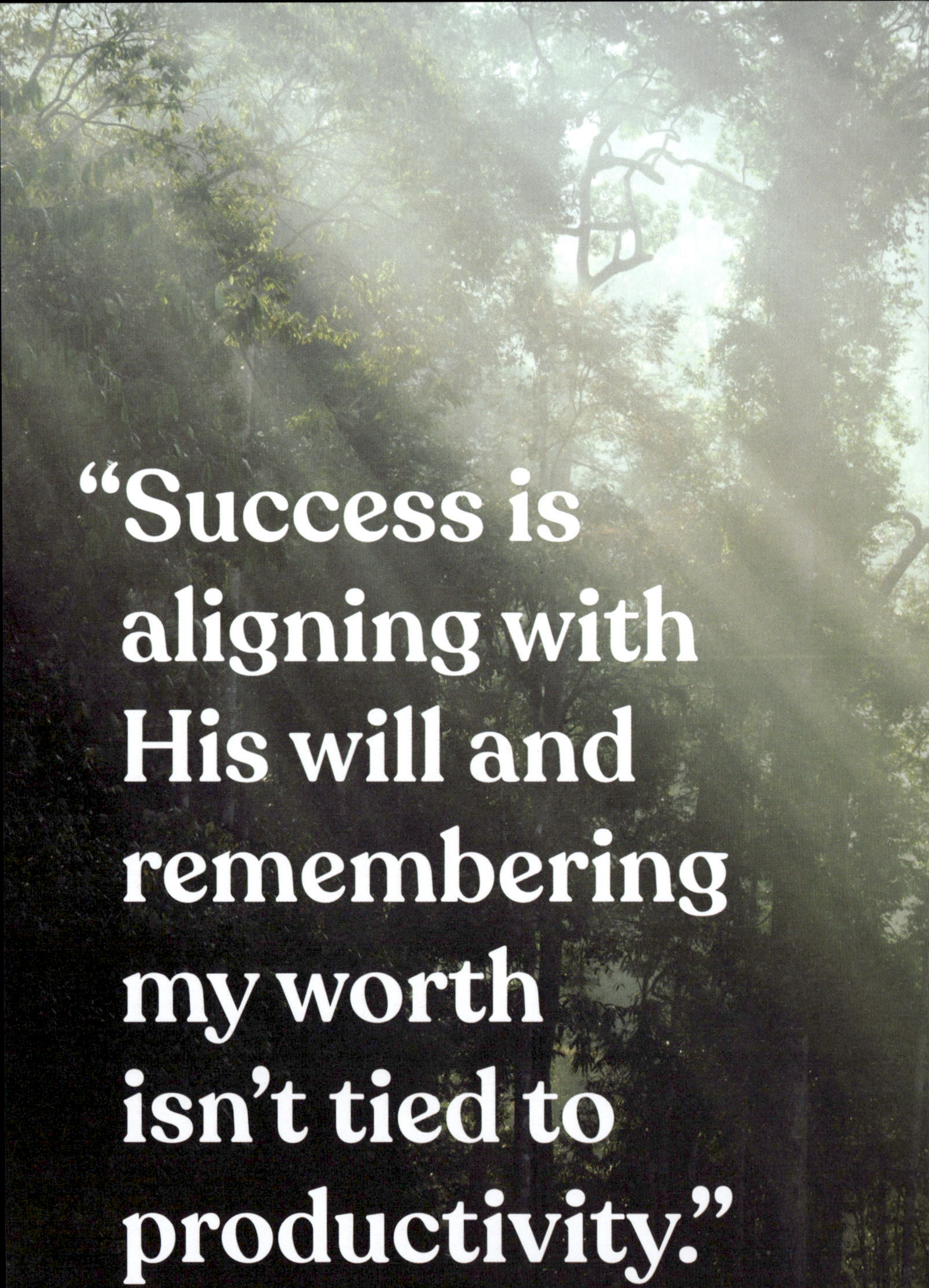

"Success is aligning with His will and remembering my worth isn't tied to productivity."

INTERVIEW 5:

Rediscovering Purpose and Identity After Career Layoff

BY: ANNIE MBRIDE ROSE
BUSINESS & COMMUNITY LEADER

1: What are you reigniting, reawakening, rediscovering, or reclaiming in this season?

A: After the arduous journey of studying to become a chemical engineer and practicing professionally for many years at a Fortune 100 company, I was laid off from my job. There were no available opportunities at other companies due to an economic downturn, and industry veterans told me I just had to "ride it out," which realistically meant waiting one to two years for commodity prices to rise so hiring could resume. This left me asking myself, *Who was I without the career I worked so hard for? Who am I if I can't be an engineer?* I had to rediscover my purpose and identity.

2: What challenges have you faced in this process, and what have they taught you?

A: As I experienced financial instability, I felt my independence and worth slip away. In my family, I consistently played the role of providing for others, which I enjoyed. I also struggled with communicating how I felt God was working in and through me. Family wanted me to take any job, but as I was learning about my purpose, I knew operating out of fear wasn't the path for me. Ultimately, staying transparent with myself, God, and loved ones helped me. I hear God most clearly when it's just me and Him, without distractions. Staying in constant prayer, fasting, and spending time in nature deepened my connection with Him.

3: What unexpected joys or revelations have come from this process?

A: I learned to trust God and others more! As a highly independent person, I had forgotten what it's like to surrender control. I saw miracles because I gave God space to operate. God revealed that sometimes either decision is okay—it's about making the choice out of faith, not fear. Perfect love casts out fear, and God is love.

4: Has this journey reshaped the way you define success or fulfillment? If so, how?

A: I no longer define success by career or finances but by my identity as a daughter of Christ. Success is aligning with His will and remembering my worth isn't tied to productivity.

5: What advice would you give someone who feels stuck in a similar rut?

A: Life is a series of chapters. Seek God for guidance, reflect on your gifts, and serve others. Trust His Word—He will lead you through.

Start Experimenting

The key to success is not in changing your situation but in changing your mindset.

— ANONYMOUS

In 2011 a man named BJ Fogg began conducting experiments in behavior change at Stanford University. Fogg's work focused on understanding how small habits could lead to lasting transformations. He discovered that making tiny, incremental changes—rather than overhauling entire routines—was the most effective way to create long-term habits.

Fogg's idea was simple: Break down a desired behavior into the smallest possible action and tie it to an existing habit. For example, instead of setting a goal to exercise for thirty minutes a day, start by committing to thirty seconds of movement, then gradually increase the time. His method, which he called the "Tiny Habits" approach, revolutionized how people thought about habit formation.

This idea of small, consistent changes aligns with II Peter 1:5–8, which urges believers to "make every effort to add to your faith goodness; and to goodness, knowledge; and to knowledge, self-control; and to self-control, perseverance; and to perseverance, godliness." These verses illustrate the power of building a strong foundation, one small step at a time. It's not about overwhelming yourself with a giant leap forward but focusing on steady progress.

Like Fogg, monthly experiments can help you transform your life by testing one new habit each month. Instead of trying to overhaul everything at once, pick a single habit to experiment with for thirty days. By narrowing your focus, you can concentrate all your energy on mastering that one habit. Whether it's drinking more water, meditating daily, or practicing gratitude each morning, the idea is to experiment and observe what works for you.

Just like Fogg's research demonstrated, the key is in making the habit achievable. For example, if you want to improve your physical health, try adding a ten-minute walk every day. At the end of the month, reflect on how it made you feel and whether it became something that stuck. If it didn't, there's no failure—only valuable insight on what might need to be adjusted.

Each month's experiment doesn't just improve your habits; it strengthens your character and deepens your walk with God. As you add to your faith through these experiments, you're building endurance, self-control, and perseverance. Every experiment is an opportunity to reflect on what is helping you grow and what is hindering your progress.

Your experiments might also offer deeper insights into God's purpose for your life. As you try different habits, you may find that certain practices draw you closer to Him, helping you cultivate virtues like patience, kindness, and humility. The goal is not perfection but progress—by intentionally testing new habits, you create space for growth and discovery, both personally and spiritually.

Monthly experiments are a powerful way to develop the habits that can help you achieve your goals and serve God in more meaningful ways. Start small, be consistent, and allow God to guide you as you experiment with new habits that will strengthen your body, mind, and spirit.

Make every effort to add to your faith goodness; and to goodness, knowledge; and to knowledge, self-control; and to self-control, perseverance; and to perseverance, godliness.

— II PETER 1:5–6

LORD,

thank You for the gift of transformation. Help me to embrace small, meaningful steps as I seek to grow in my habits and walk closer with You. Guide me in discovering the changes that align with Your purpose for my life. Give me the perseverance to stay committed and the wisdom to learn from every step of this journey.

AMEN.

QUESTIONS TO CONSIDER:

1. What is one small change you've been thinking about making in your life?
2. How can you break that change into a smaller, more manageable step to start today?
3. How have small, consistent habits helped you grow in the past?
4. Are there any habits you've been holding onto that no longer serve God's purpose for your life?
5. How can experimenting with new habits deepen your relationship with God and others?

RIGHT NOW:

- Write down one habit you'd like to experiment with this month and break it into the smallest possible starting point, e.g., if your goal is to drink more water, commit to drinking one extra glass a day.

THIS WEEK:

- Test your new habit daily for the next week. Record how it makes you feel, any challenges you encounter, and any changes you notice, no matter how small.
- Reflect on what God is teaching you through this process.

MOVING FORWARD:

- Expand your experiment. If the habit is working for you, increase it slightly—for example, move from one extra glass of water to two, or from a five-minute walk to a ten-minute walk.
- At the end of the month, review your progress. Did this habit positively impact your life? If so, consider keeping it or building upon it. If not, think about what adjustments you might make.
- Make a list of other habits or disciplines you'd like to experiment with. Pray for God's guidance as you choose your next focus.

Reminder:

Transformation doesn't come from massive leaps—it comes from small, consistent steps made in faith. You're not aiming for perfection; you're building a life aligned with God's purpose, one habit at a time.

Create Action Triggers

Success doesn't come from what you do occasionally,
but from what you do consistently.

— MARIE FORLEO

Once you've begun experimenting with new habits—one at a time, as BJ Fogg's research recommends—the next step is to make those habits stick. How? By linking them to routines you already have in place. This method, often called creating "action triggers," takes something familiar and pairs it with the new behavior, allowing the new habit to feel natural over time.

Consider how Fogg's approach works: You take an existing habit, like brushing your teeth, and anchor a new habit to it. For example, if your monthly experiment was to start practicing gratitude, you could decide to name three things you're thankful for every time you brush your teeth. The physical act of brushing becomes the trigger for your new practice. By pairing the two, you strengthen the new habit without adding complexity to your day.

First Timothy 4:7 (ESV) encourages us to "discipline yourself for the purpose of godliness." This discipline isn't about rigid rules but about building intentional routines that help us grow in faith and character. Action triggers can serve as a practical way to infuse your day with purpose, reminding you of the spiritual habits and practices you want to cultivate.

Behavioral scientists have found that habits tied to existing routines are more likely to become automatic. For instance, people who set a habit of exercising right after their morning coffee or devotional time often find it easier to stick with their routine. The brain associates the trigger—in this case, the morning coffee—with the action, making the new habit feel less forced and more natural.

Think of action triggers as a bridge between the habits you're experimenting with and the life you're striving to create. The key is to start small and be specific. For instance, instead of saying, "I'll pray more," decide to pray for one minute while your coffee brews. Instead of "I'll be more active," plan to do ten squats every time you wait for the microwave. If your goal is to become a better friend, send a text to someone every time you go to the restroom. These small, consistent cues help the habit take root, making it part of the rhythm of your day. By pairing these actions with existing routines, you reduce the mental effort required and make the habit easier to sustain.

As you move from experimenting with new habits to integrating them into your daily life, let action triggers be your guide. They're not just tools for habit formation; they're reminders of the purposeful, God-centered life you're building. With each trigger, you're not just creating new routines—you're cultivating a life that reflects discipline, intentionality, and faithfulness.

Discipline yourself for the purpose of godliness.

— I TIMOTHY 4:7 NASB

LORD,

thank You for the gift of discipline and the opportunity to grow closer to You through intentional habits. Help me to see the moments in my day where I can anchor my actions to routines that honor You. Give me the strength to remain consistent and the faith to trust that these small steps will lead to greater transformation.

AMEN.

QUESTIONS TO CONSIDER:

1. What is a new habit you've recently started or would like to start?
2. What existing routine or daily action could serve as a trigger for this habit?
3. How can this habit bring you closer to God or reflect His purpose for your life?
4. Are there specific times of day when you feel most focused and capable of building new habits?
5. How will you remind yourself to stay consistent in linking your action trigger to the new habit?

RIGHT NOW:

- Identify one habit you want to anchor with an action trigger. Write it down and choose an existing routine to pair it with (e.g., practicing gratitude while brushing your teeth).
- Test the action trigger today. Pair the new habit with the routine.

THIS WEEK:

- Practice your new habit daily, tied to the same action trigger each time. For instance, if you want to meditate, do so right after pouring your morning coffee.
- Reflect at the end of the week on how the action trigger helped you stay consistent. Did it fit naturally into your day?

MOVING FORWARD:

- Expand your use of action triggers by identifying additional habits you want to cultivate. Pair each with a specific routine.
- Adjust and refine your triggers as needed. If one isn't working, try another routine to anchor the habit more effectively.
- Build a habit-tracking system to see how well you're maintaining your routines. Celebrate small wins along the way.

Reminder:

Small, intentional habits tied to everyday moments create a ripple effect that shapes your life and reflects God's purpose for you. Consistency, not perfection, is the goal.

Write Your "No" List

You have to make room for the life you want.

— OPRAH WINFREY

In the early 2000s, Oprah Winfrey made headlines when she publicly declared that she would no longer accept toxic people in her life. After years of navigating personal and professional challenges, Oprah shared that she had learned the importance of setting boundaries. For her, the "no" was as powerful as the "yes." She explained that it was essential to prioritize what mattered most to her and eliminate distractions and negative influences that drained her energy. By setting firm boundaries, she made room for the relationships and opportunities that truly nourished her.

This mindset of eliminating what no longer serves aligns with the teaching of Jesus in Matthew 5:37: All you need to say is simply 'Yes' or 'No'; anything beyond this comes from the evil one." Jesus calls His followers to clarity and decisiveness in their choices. When you say no, you are protecting your time, energy, and purpose. It's a declaration of self-respect, one that ensures you don't lose yourself in the demands of others.

Oprah's choice to set boundaries wasn't just about removing people from her life—it was a conscious decision to honor her own worth and make room for what aligned with her values. Her ability to say no to distractions allowed her to focus on her health, relationships, and creative endeavors. She understood that sometimes the best thing you can do for your future is to say no to what doesn't serve you.

Studies in psychology reveal that setting boundaries is not only essential for mental well-being, but it also leads to higher self-esteem and improved productivity. Research from the University of Rochester Medical Center highlights that establishing healthy boundaries, including being comfortable with saying no, is a key strategy for preventing burnout and maintaining emotional well-being. They are also more likely to feel fulfilled in their personal and professional lives because they make intentional decisions that align with their goals.

As you create your own "No List," ask yourself: *What am I allowing in my life that doesn't align with my values or purpose?* It could be toxic relationships, draining commitments, or unnecessary obligations that pull you away from your higher calling. Saying no is a skill that requires practice and discernment, but it's one that is essential for personal growth and spiritual well-being.

The Bible also encourages us to guard our hearts and minds (Proverbs 4:23), and sometimes that means eliminating negative influences and environments. Saying no to what doesn't serve your higher purpose opens space for greater focus, peace, and clarity. It's not about rejecting others but about making room for the things that honor who you truly are and who God has called you to be.

By creating a "No List," you are taking an active role in designing the life you want. You are setting healthy boundaries that protect your mental, emotional, and spiritual well-being. This practice will help you remain steadfast in your mission and allow you to say yes to the things that truly matter.

> **All you need to say is simply "Yes" or "No"; anything beyond this comes from the evil one.**
>
> — MATTHEW 5:37

LORD,

thank You for the clarity and wisdom You provide in every decision. Help me to discern what aligns with Your will for my life and give me the courage to say no when necessary. Protect my heart and mind from distractions and guide me to use my time and energy for Your glory.

AMEN.

QUESTIONS TO CONSIDER:

1. What commitments or relationships in your life feel draining or misaligned with your values?
2. Are there any habits or routines you need to say no to in order to focus on your purpose?
3. How does fear of disappointing others influence your decisions to say yes?
4. What would making space for the things that truly nourish you look like in practice?
5. How can setting boundaries bring you closer to fulfilling God's calling for your life?

RIGHT NOW:

- Identify one area of your life where you feel overwhelmed or distracted. Write down at least one thing you need to say no to immediately.
- Reflect on how saying no to this one thing can open space for greater peace and focus.

THIS WEEK:

- Create your own "No List." Write down specific people, commitments, or habits that no longer align with your values and purpose.
- Practice saying no to one unnecessary obligation or commitment. Pay attention to how it feels to set that boundary and the relief or clarity it brings.

MOVING FORWARD:

- Review and refine your "No List" regularly. As new opportunities and demands arise, compare them to your values and goals.
- Develop a clear framework for decision-making. Ask yourself: *Does this serve my calling and bring me closer to God's purpose for my life?*
- Communicate your boundaries with grace and firmness, ensuring that others respect the priorities you've set for yourself.

Reminder:

Saying no to what drains you is saying yes to the peace, purpose, and joy God has prepared for you.

Excavate Your Plans

The best way to predict the future is to create it.

— ABRAHAM LINCOLN

It's easy to think of innovation as something brand new—a fresh idea, an uncharted direction, a blank canvas ready for creation. But sometimes the greatest breakthroughs aren't about starting from scratch; they're about revisiting, reclaiming, and refining what was left behind.

Isaiah 43:18–19 reminds us of God's power to renew and restore: "Forget the former things; do not dwell on the past. See, I am doing a new thing! Now it springs up; do you not perceive it? I am making a way in the wilderness and streams in the wasteland." This passage isn't about erasing the past—it's about God's ability to breathe new life into what once seemed barren. Similarly, some of the best ideas and opportunities in your life may be hidden in projects or dreams you thought were long dead.

Consider the story of Ava DuVernay, the visionary filmmaker behind *Selma* and *When They See Us*. Before rising to prominence, she built a career in public relations, founding her own agency while nurturing a deep love for storytelling. Though she was drawn to filmmaking, she initially saw it as an inaccessible path due to the industry's systemic barriers. Still, the desire lingered. Instead of abandoning the idea, she began revisiting her aspirations in small, experimental ways—first by making short films on a shoestring budget. What seemed like an old, unattainable dream became the foundation for an extraordinary career.

Ava's story is a testament to how revisiting and reshaping old ideas can lead to profound transformation.

In your life, there may be dreams you've buried under the weight of time, fear, or failure. Perhaps there's a business idea that didn't take off the first time, a creative project you abandoned, or a passion you shelved because life got in the way. "Project Archaeology" invites you to dig through those old ideas and assess their value. What could be dusted off and given a second chance? What lessons have you learned since then that could breathe fresh life into what once felt stale?

This isn't about clinging to the past. It's about partnering with God to reimagine it. Isaiah's words remind us that God specializes in making a way where there seems to be none. He turns deserts into streams and forgotten dreams into flourishing realities. If you're willing to revisit and rework, what once seemed impossible might become the very thing God uses to bless others and glorify His name.

So, where do you begin? Start by taking inventory. Write down old ideas, projects, or dreams that still tug at your heart. Ask yourself: *What made me passionate about this in the first place? What stopped me from pursuing it? And most importantly, how has God equipped me now in ways I wasn't ready before?* By prayerfully revisiting these questions, you may uncover buried treasures that God is ready to refine and revive.

Remember, progress isn't always about moving forward. Sometimes it's about looking back with fresh eyes and a heart open to God's renewing power. Just as Ava DuVernay discovered her true calling by revisiting an old passion, you too can unearth something beautiful and life-giving when you take the time to dig.

Forget the former things; do not dwell on the past. See, I am doing a new thing! Now it springs up; do you not perceive it? I am making a way in the wilderness and streams in the wasteland.

— ISAIAH 43:18–19

LORD,
thank You for Your ability to renew and restore. Help me to see with fresh eyes the dreams and plans You've planted in my heart. Give me courage to revisit what I've left behind, discernment to know what to refine, and faith to trust Your timing and provision.
AMEN.

QUESTIONS TO CONSIDER:

1. Are there any dreams or projects from your past that still tug at your heart?
2. What stopped you from pursuing them the first time, and how have you grown since then?
3. How might God be calling you to revisit and refine these ideas in this season of your life?
4. Are there lessons from past failures or setbacks that can guide your next steps?
5. How can prayer and reflection help you discern which plans to excavate and which to leave behind?

RIGHT NOW:

- Write down three past ideas, dreams, or projects that still hold meaning for you. Pray over each one, asking God to reveal if they are worth revisiting and refining.
- Reflect on what initially inspired these ideas and what stopped you from pursuing them further.

THIS WEEK:

- Choose one idea from your list to explore further. Write a short plan outlining what it would look like to rework or revisit this dream with your current skills, knowledge, and resources.
- Schedule time to take one small, tangible step toward reviving that dream, such as researching, brainstorming, or seeking advice.

MOVING FORWARD:

- Make "Project Archaeology" a regular practice. Set aside time each month to revisit past ideas and assess their potential with prayer and reflection.
- Create a system for capturing and organizing ideas as they come, so nothing is forgotten or lost over time.
- Continually seek God's guidance, allowing Him to shape your plans and show you how they fit into His purpose for your life.

Reminder:
God specializes in renewing and restoring what once seemed lost. Trust Him to turn your forgotten dreams into flourishing realities.

Set Your Standards

Success is not final, failure is not fatal:

It is the courage to continue that counts.

— WINSTON CHURCHILL

In the late 1990s, Serena Williams was a young tennis prodigy with dreams of greatness. While her natural talent and rigorous training were essential, what truly set Serena apart was her unique way of defining success. Early in her career, Serena shared that her personal metrics of achievement didn't always align with the standard wins and losses recorded on paper. Instead, she focused on the lessons learned after each match, how well she had applied her strategies, and whether she had given her absolute best effort. For Serena, success wasn't just about trophies; it was about consistent growth.

This mindset helped her overcome setbacks, including injuries and losses, that could have derailed her career. Instead of being discouraged by a defeat, she would ask herself, *Did I play better than the last time? What can I improve? Did I stay focused on my goals?* These questions, rooted in personal accountability and continuous improvement, allowed her to rise above external validation and concentrate on her own journey.

This concept ties wonderfully to the words of II Peter 3:18: "But grow in the grace and knowledge of our Lord and Savior Jesus Christ. To him be glory both now and forever! Amen." Growth, as Peter reminds us, is not a one-time event but a continual process of becoming more aligned with God's purpose for our lives. When we measure success by how we grow spiritually, mentally, and emotionally, rather than by society's standards, we unlock a deeper sense of fulfillment.

Serena's story teaches us the importance of defining our own personal metrics of success. For some, success may mean deepening relationships or cultivating inner peace. For others, it may involve honing a skill or stepping out in faith to pursue a new opportunity. The key is to determine what matters most to you and to measure your progress based on those unique values, rather than comparing yourself to others.

Studies in psychology support the idea that intrinsic goals—those rooted in personal growth, relationships, and meaningful contributions—lead to greater well-being than extrinsic goals like wealth or fame. When we define success in ways that resonate with our core beliefs and values, we are more likely to experience joy and purpose in our pursuits.

Take time to reflect on what success looks like for you. Is it about building a closer relationship with God? Improving your health? Writing that book you've been dreaming of? Whatever it is, create personal metrics that align with your God-given purpose, and keep track of your progress. As you do, remember that growth is a journey, not a destination.

Just like Serena Williams, you have the power to redefine success on your own terms. By focusing on progress rather than perfection, you can cultivate a life of intentionality, joy, and lasting impact.

But grow in the grace and knowledge of our Lord and Savior Jesus Christ. To Him be glory both now and forever! Amen.

— II PETER 3:18

LORD,

help me to redefine success according to Your will for my life. Teach me to seek growth in grace and knowledge, and to measure my progress by how well I am walking in alignment with You. Free me from the pressure of comparison and the need for external validation, so I can focus on becoming the person You've called me to be.

AMEN.

QUESTIONS TO CONSIDER:

1. How have you been measuring success in your life so far? Does it align with your values and purpose?
2. What lessons have you learned from setbacks or failures that have helped you grow?
3. How can you shift your focus from external validation to intrinsic goals like personal growth and spiritual maturity?
4. What are three specific areas of your life where you want to see progress?
5. How can you incorporate God's grace into your definition of success?

RIGHT NOW:

- Write down your current definition of success. Then, reflect on whether it aligns with your values and God's purpose for your life.
- Identify one area where you've been comparing yourself to others, and release it to God in prayer.

THIS WEEK:

- Create a list of personal metrics for success based on your values. These could include things like growing in faith, improving a skill, or deepening relationships.
- Track one action each day that moves you closer to success according to your personal metrics.

MOVING FORWARD:

- Make a habit of evaluating your progress weekly. Ask yourself: *Am I growing in the areas that matter most to me?*
- Regularly revisit your definition of success and adjust it as needed to stay aligned with your values and God's calling.
- Celebrate small wins as markers of growth, not just milestones of completion.

Reminder:

True success isn't about perfection; it's about growing in grace, knowledge, and alignment with God's purpose for your life. Keep pressing forward with courage.

Face Your Excuses

Excuses are the lies we tell ourselves so that it doesn't have to be our fault.

— JENNA ANISTON

When Shonda Rhimes declared her "Year of Yes," she committed to breaking out of her comfort zone. Despite her remarkable success as a television producer, she admitted in her memoir that she had built a fortress of excuses to avoid new challenges. "I'm too busy," "I don't have time," and "I'm not that kind of person" were excuses that kept her from fully engaging with life outside of her work. One day, her sister casually remarked, "You never say yes to anything," and it was the wake-up call she needed.

Rhimes decided to confront her excuses head-on. She wrote them down, and rewrote them as deliberate choices:

- "I don't have time" became "I choose to spend my time differently."
- "I'm too introverted" became "I choose to let fear of discomfort dictate my actions."
- "I'm not a public speaker" became "I choose not to develop that skill."

This simple but profound exercise forced her to own her decisions instead of hiding behind excuses. The result? She stepped into experiences that ultimately transformed her, such as delivering beautiful commencement speeches and intentionally playing with her kids.

The Bible reminds us in Romans 14:12 that we will all "give an account of ourselves to God." This verse isn't about judgment but about responsibility. When we cling to excuses, we deny ourselves the opportunity to grow, and we miss out on the abundant life God has planned for us. Writing down your excuses, as Shonda did, allows you to see them for what they are—barriers you've created that prevent you from stepping into your purpose.

Psychologists call this reframing. Reframing your thoughts can shift your mindset, turning obstacles into opportunities for growth. For example, research published in the journal *Behavior Research and Therapy* highlights how cognitive restructuring helps individuals overcome self-imposed limitations. By consciously shifting your narrative from "I can't" to "I choose not to," you empower yourself to make deliberate, purpose-driven decisions.

Take a moment to reflect on your own life. Write down the excuses you have been holding onto, and rewrite each as a conscious choice:

- "I don't have enough time" might become "I choose to prioritize other things over this."
- "I'm not talented enough" might become "I choose not to invest in learning and growth."
- "I've tried and failed before" might become "I choose not to try again because failure scares me."

This practice isn't about self-condemnation—it's about reclaiming your agency. It's about aligning your choices with your God-given purpose and taking responsibility for the life you're called to live.

So then, each of us will give an account of ourselves to God.

— ROMANS 14:12

LORD,
help me to see my excuses for what they are—
barriers I've created that keep me from fully stepping into
Your purpose for my life. Give me the courage to confront them,
reframe them, and take responsibility for my actions.
I ask for Your guidance and strength as I move forward in faith,
trusting in Your plan for my growth and transformation.
AMEN.

QUESTIONS TO CONSIDER:

1. What recurring excuses do you find yourself using, and how have they held you back?
2. When have you allowed fear or discomfort to dictate your choices?
3. How can you reframe your excuses into deliberate, purposeful decisions?
4. What would your life look like if you stopped allowing excuses to control your actions?
5. How can you invite God into the process of overcoming your self-imposed limitations?

RIGHT NOW:

- Write down three excuses you've been holding onto.
- Reframe each one as a deliberate choice, following Shonda Rhimes's example.

THIS WEEK:

- Track how often you catch yourself making excuses. Write them down as they arise and reframe them in the moment.
- Identify one small action step you can take to challenge an excuse and demonstrate accountability.

MOVING FORWARD:

- Create a habit of self-reflection at the end of each week. Ask yourself: *What excuses did I make, and how did I overcome them?*
- Share your reframed excuses with a trusted friend or mentor for encouragement and accountability.
- Pray daily for God to reveal areas where excuses have been holding you back and for His strength to move forward.

Reminder:

Excuses are just barriers you've created—but God has given you the power to break through them and step boldly into your purpose. Take responsibility, trust His plan, and move forward in faith.

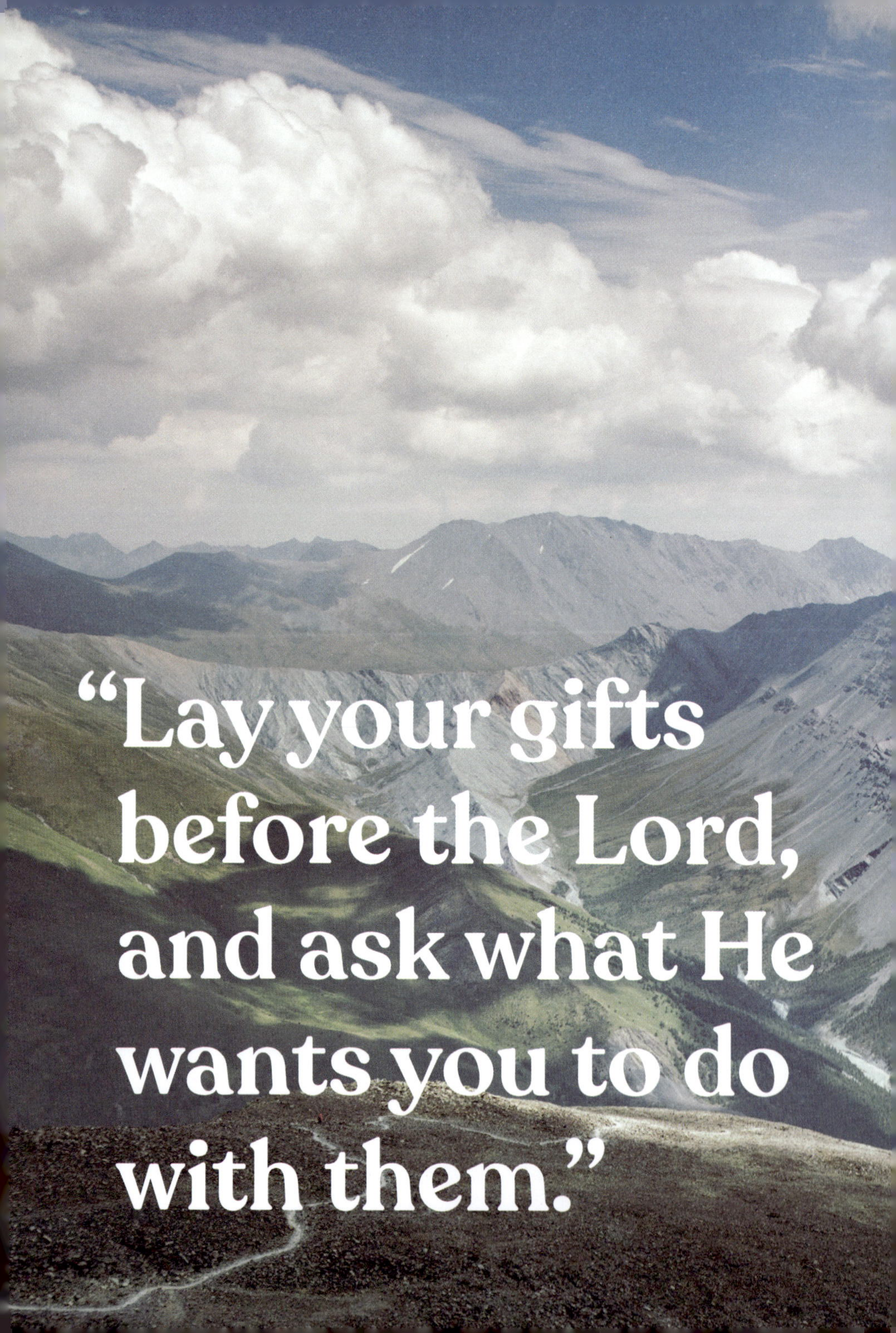
"Lay your gifts
before the Lord,
and ask what He
wants you to do
with them."

INTERVIEW 6:

Reigniting Creativity

BY MEGAN J. CONNER
AUTHOR | EDITOR

1: What are you reigniting, reawakening, rediscovering, or reclaiming in this season?

A: I am passionate about reigniting and reclaiming our creativity as offerings back to the Great Artist. I spent years working in the creative arts until the Lord revealed it had become an idol. I unintentionally replaced my First Love. Understanding this, I completed all directorial, performance, or writing obligations and laid it all down, certain I would never work as a creative again. I walked away—full stop! Nearly fifteen years later, God brought back those gifts in ways I never could have imagined.

2: What challenges have you faced in this process, and what have they taught you?

A: As a believer working in this space, I've faced immense criticism, efforts to thwart my participation, and even persecution. However, my greatest challenges weren't external—they were internal. The heart is deceitful, and the slippery slope of pride or self-sufficiency can beguile even the strongest believers. After years away from this work, surrender and humility have become my constant guides. I've learned God grants us "talents" to use, not hide. I long to hear, "Well done, good and faithful servant" (Matthew 25:23). To do this, I must step out in faith, anchor myself to Him, and create for His delight and purposes.

3: What unexpected joys or revelations have come from this process?

A: At eighteen, I dreamed of founding a Christian theater company, though such entities barely existed then. I never told a soul. Almost twenty years later, I had the opportunity to create one in the most unique way. God reminded me how He sees the secret places in our hearts.

4: Has this journey reshaped the way you define success or fulfillment? If so, how?

A: When I was younger, success meant visibility. Now, I define success as obedience. I no longer claw or hustle for opportunity; I let God lead me. Every project is a sacrifice laid on the altar. What happens after is up to Him.

5: What advice would you give someone who feels stuck in a similar rut?

A: Surrender. Lay your gifts before the Lord, and ask what He wants you to do with them. You cannot bury your talents. God formed you to create. So go . . . CREATE!

Do a Relationship Audit

You are the average of the five people you spend the most time with.

— JIM ROHN

In 1955 Rosa Parks made a decision that would change the course of history when she refused to give up her seat on a Montgomery bus. Her quiet courage sparked the Civil Rights Movement, but Parks didn't act alone. Her strength came, in part, from the community around her—mentors, friends, and leaders who shared her vision for justice and equality. Among them were figures like Martin Luther King Jr., E. D. Nixon, and Jo Ann Robinson, who supported and encouraged her actions. Parks's story reminds us that relationships can either uplift us toward our purpose or hinder us from achieving it.

Hebrews 10:24–25 says, "Let us consider how we may spur one another on toward love and good deeds, not giving up meeting together, as some are in the habit of doing, but encouraging one another—and all the more as you see the Day approaching." This verse underscores the importance of surrounding ourselves with people who inspire and encourage us in our faith and purpose.

Conducting a relationship audit means taking an honest look at the connections in your life. Are they helping you grow, or are they pulling you away from the person God is calling you to be? This doesn't mean cutting people off harshly but rather setting boundaries that protect your emotional, spiritual, and mental well-being.

Psychologists have long studied the impact of relationships on well-being, and the findings are clear: The people you spend the most time with significantly influence your habits, mindset, and even your happiness. Toxic relationships can drain your energy and focus, while uplifting relationships can propel you toward your goals.

Start your audit by categorizing your relationships into three groups: those who pour into you, those you pour into, and those that feel draining. Reflect on how much time and energy you're dedicating to each group. Are there imbalances that need to be addressed? Perhaps you're giving too much to relationships that leave you feeling depleted or not investing enough in those that bring you joy and growth.

Rosa Parks's story also reminds us of the importance of community. As you conduct your audit, consider whether you have a circle of people who challenge you, encourage you, and share your values. If not, ask God to bring those relationships into your life. Sometimes building meaningful connections requires stepping out of your comfort zone and seeking new communities.

A relationship audit isn't just about evaluating others; it's also an opportunity to reflect on your own role in relationships. Are you encouraging others, or are you unintentionally contributing to negativity? Are you a source of love and good deeds, as Hebrews calls us to be?

By taking the time to evaluate your connections and set healthy boundaries, you create space for relationships that align with your purpose and strengthen your faith. Surround yourself with those who spur you on, and strive to be that person for others. In doing so, you'll cultivate a network of love, support, and encouragement that reflects God's design for community.

> **Let us consider how we may spur one another on toward love and good deeds, not giving up meeting together . . . but encouraging one another.**
>
> — HEBREWS 10:24–25

LORD,

thank You for the people You've placed in my life. Help me to evaluate my relationships with wisdom and love, setting boundaries where needed and investing in connections that honor You. Teach me to be a source of encouragement and strength for others, and guide me in building a community that reflects Your love and purpose.

AMEN.

QUESTIONS TO CONSIDER:

1. Who in your life pours into you, and how do they encourage your growth?
2. Are there relationships that leave you feeling drained or discouraged?
3. How can you set healthy boundaries with those who may not align with your purpose?
4. Do you have a community that challenges and supports you in your faith and calling?
5. How can you become a source of encouragement and strength for others?

RIGHT NOW:

- Make a list of the people you spend the most time with, and categorize them into three groups: those who pour into you, those you pour into, and those who drain you.
- Identify one relationship in each category and pray for God's guidance on how to nurture, maintain, or set boundaries within that connection.

THIS WEEK:

- Reach out to someone who pours into you, and express your gratitude for their presence in your life.
- Identify one boundary you can set in a draining relationship, and take a small step to implement it with kindness and grace.
- Plan an intentional time to connect with someone who encourages you, whether through a phone call, coffee date, or shared activity.

MOVING FORWARD:

- Regularly review your relationships to ensure they align with your values and purpose.
- Seek opportunities to expand your circle with people who inspire and challenge you in your faith.
- Commit to being a positive influence in the lives of others by offering encouragement, love, and support.

Reminder:

The people in your life shape your path. Choose wisely, set boundaries boldly, and nurture relationships that reflect God's love and purpose.

Plan Your Progress

Education is the most powerful weapon which you can use to change the world.

— NELSON MANDELA

Malala Yousafzai's journey is a testament to the power of intentional, focused learning. After surviving an attack by the Taliban for advocating for girls' education, Malala refused to let fear or adversity derail her dreams. Instead, she created a clear vision for her education and future, pursuing each step with purpose and determination. From completing her secondary education in the UK to earning her degree at Oxford University, Malala's life demonstrates what is possible when you set intentional goals and follow a roadmap to achieve them.

Malala's story reflects the wisdom of II Peter 1:5–6, which urges believers to "make every effort to add to your faith goodness; and to goodness, knowledge; and to knowledge, self-control; and to self-control, perseverance." Spiritual growth, like skill development, often requires a deliberate process. By breaking your goals into achievable steps, you create a roadmap that not only helps you stay on track but also deepens your faith and character along the way.

Creating a learning roadmap starts with identifying what you want to learn and why. Malala's mission to advocate for education fueled her commitment to acquiring knowledge. Similarly, your roadmap should align with your purpose and passions. Whether you're learning a new skill for work, deepening your spiritual knowledge, or pursuing a creative hobby, the key is to focus your efforts within a specific time frame.

Experts in goal setting recommend dividing learning into ninety-day sprints. This approach provides enough time to make meaningful progress without feeling overwhelmed. For example, if your goal is to learn a new language, your first ninety-day sprint might focus on mastering basic vocabulary and phrases.

Malala's story also reminds us of the importance of persistence and flexibility. Despite numerous obstacles, she adapted her roadmap to fit her changing circumstances, always keeping her ultimate goal in sight. As you create your learning roadmap, leave room for adjustments. Life is unpredictable, but with a clear plan, you can navigate challenges without losing sight of your destination.

Science supports the effectiveness of structured learning plans. Observations suggest that setting specific, time-bound goals increases motivation and retention. The act of planning your learning process helps you focus your energy and track your progress, making it more likely that you'll stick with your goals over time.

As you embark on your learning journey, invite God into the process. Ask Him to guide your steps and reveal the skills and knowledge He wants you to develop. Remember, your learning isn't just for personal gain; it's an opportunity to serve others and glorify God.

By creating a learning roadmap, you're not just acquiring new skills—you're building a foundation for lasting growth and impact. Take the first step, set your sights on the next ninety days, and trust that God will lead you toward the purpose He has for your life.

Make every effort to add to your faith goodness; and to goodness, knowledge; and to knowledge, self-control; and to self-control, perseverance.

— II PETER 1:5–6

LORD,

thank You for giving me the ability to learn and grow. Guide my steps as I set goals and pursue knowledge. Help me stay focused and motivated, and remind me that all my efforts are for Your glory and to serve others. Give me perseverance when the path is challenging and wisdom to adjust when needed.

AMEN.

QUESTIONS TO CONSIDER:

1. What is one skill, area of knowledge, or practice you feel God is calling you to grow in?
2. How does this goal align with your larger purpose or passion?
3. What obstacles or challenges might you face as you pursue this learning journey?
4. What small, actionable steps can you take in the next ninety days to make progress?
5. How can you use this growth to serve others and glorify God?

RIGHT NOW:

- Write down one specific goal you want to achieve in the next ninety days. Make it clear and measurable (e.g., "Learn one hundred new vocabulary words in Spanish" or "Complete a beginner's drawing course").
- Identify the resources you'll need to get started (e.g., books, online courses, mentors, tools).

THIS WEEK:

- Break your goal into smaller milestones. For example, divide a ninety-day goal into weekly or biweekly tasks.
- Set aside specific times during the week for learning or practice. Block it into your calendar and treat it as a priority.
- Reach out to someone who can support or guide you—whether it's a mentor, accountability partner, or coach.

MOVING FORWARD:

- Review your progress weekly. Celebrate small wins and adjust your roadmap if needed.
- Reflect on what God is teaching you during this process, and document it in a journal or prayer log.
- Begin thinking about how you can use your new skills or knowledge to positively impact others, whether in your personal life, community, or workplace.

Reminder:

Progress isn't about perfection—it's about showing up, staying consistent, and trusting that each step brings you closer to God's purpose for your life.

Start a Solution Log

Problems are not stop signs, they are guidelines.

— ROBERT H. SCHULLER

George Washington Carver, one of history's most brilliant problem solvers, built his legacy through innovative thinking and meticulous documentation. Born into slavery and raised during a time of limited opportunity for Black Americans, Carver's determination to find solutions propelled him to become a world-renowned agricultural scientist. His work transformed Southern agriculture, providing sustainable practices that revitalized depleted soil and helped struggling farmers thrive.

Carver's most famous contributions involved peanuts and sweet potatoes. While many know of his inventions—everything from peanut-based wood stains to alternative fuels—few realize the methodical problem-solving that went into his discoveries. Carver faced challenges head-on, asking questions like, "What can I do with this crop?" and "How can it benefit people and the land?" He documented his processes carefully, experimenting and refining ideas until he arrived at solutions that worked.

Proverbs 3:13–14 (ESV) reminds us, "Blessed is the one who finds wisdom, and the one who gets understanding, for the gain from her is better than gain from silver and her profit better than gold." Carver's life illustrates this truth: Wisdom is found not in avoiding problems but in addressing them with faith, creativity, and persistence. His careful documentation not only helped him solve immediate challenges but also allowed his findings to benefit countless others.

Starting a "solution log" is a practical way to adopt Carver's approach. It's about creating a record of how you tackle problems—big or small. Whether it's overcoming a personal obstacle, managing a work project, or resolving a relational issue, documenting your process helps you learn from experience and build a tool kit for future challenges.

Researchers have found that journaling about problem-solving enhances critical thinking and decision-making skills. By reflecting on what worked and what didn't, you can refine your approach and develop strategies that are more effective over time.

Carver's solution-focused mindset also offers a spiritual lesson. He saw his work as an act of worship, often saying, "I love to think of nature as an unlimited broadcasting station, through which God speaks to us every hour, if we will only tune in." His faith was woven into his problem-solving, and he sought God's wisdom in his experiments. In the same way, starting a solution log can become a spiritual practice, inviting God into your challenges and reflecting on His guidance and provision.

Begin by identifying a current problem or challenge. Write it down, along with possible solutions and the steps you're taking to address it. As you work through the problem, update your log with what you learn along the way. Over time, your solution log will become a valuable resource, reminding you of God's faithfulness and your capacity to grow through challenges.

George Washington Carver's story reminds us that problems are opportunities in disguise. By approaching them with intentionality and faith, you can not only overcome them but also create solutions that bless others.

Blessed is the one who finds wisdom, and the one who gets understanding, for the gain from her is better than gain from silver and her profit better than gold.

— PROVERBS 3:13–14 (ESV)

LORD,

thank You for the wisdom You provide in every situation. Help me to approach challenges with faith, creativity, and persistence. Teach me to see problems as opportunities for growth and to rely on Your guidance as I seek solutions. May my efforts glorify You and bless others.

AMEN.

QUESTIONS TO CONSIDER:

1. What challenges or problems are you currently facing in your life, work, or relationships?
2. How have you successfully overcome similar challenges in the past?
3. What lessons can you take from Scripture or prayer to apply to this situation?
4. Are there steps you can take today to start addressing this issue?
5. How can documenting this process help you learn and grow for the future?

RIGHT NOW:

- Identify one specific problem or challenge you're currently facing.
- Start your solution log by writing down the problem and brainstorming at least three potential solutions or approaches.
- Pray over the situation, asking God to guide you.

THIS WEEK:

- Act on at least one of the solutions you brainstormed. Document the steps you take, any obstacles you encounter, and the results.
- Reflect daily on what you're learning from the process, and update your solution log with insights or adjustments.
- Seek advice or support from someone who has faced a similar challenge or has expertise in the area.

MOVING FORWARD:

- Make it a habit to document challenges and solutions in your log regularly. Over time, review past entries to identify patterns or strategies that have worked well for you.
- Use your log as a tool for personal and spiritual growth by including notes about how God has shown up in your problem-solving journey.
- Share a solution or lesson you've learned with someone who may benefit from it, turning your challenge into a blessing for others.

Reminder:

Every problem is an opportunity for growth and deeper reliance on God. Trust that He will guide you to solutions that glorify Him and strengthen you.

Create a Fear List

I learned that courage was not the absence of fear, but the triumph over it.

— NELSON MANDELA

Fear has a way of clouding our vision, making obstacles seem larger than they truly are. It whispers lies that paralyze us, convincing us to stay in our comfort zones rather than step into the unknown. But what if we could strip fear of its power by naming it, examining it, and putting it in perspective?

Nelson Mandela, one of the world's most iconic leaders, understood the reality of fear intimately. During his twenty-seven years of imprisonment, he faced uncertainty, isolation, and immense physical and emotional challenges. Yet Mandela chose not to let fear dictate his actions. Instead, he dissected it. He acknowledged the risks and realities, but he refused to let fear have the final say. His ability to assess fear's likelihood and impact allowed him to move forward with courage, ultimately transforming his life and the history of South Africa.

Isaiah 41:10 offers us divine reassurance: "So do not fear, for I am with you; do not be dismayed, for I am your God. I will strengthen you and help you; I will uphold you with My righteous right hand." This verse reminds us that while fear is a natural human emotion, it does not have to control us. When we bring our fears into the light of God's presence, we can see them for what they truly are—often less overwhelming than they first appeared.

Creating a Fear List is a powerful way to confront and diminish fear.

Begin by listing your current fears, whether they're related to work, relationships, health, or your spiritual journey. Next to each fear, rate its likelihood on a scale from 1 to 10. How probable is it that this fear will actually come to pass? Then, assess its potential impact—if the fear did become reality, how severe would the consequences be? Often, this exercise reveals that many fears are either unlikely or not as catastrophic as we'd imagined.

Mandela's approach to fear reflects this process. He didn't ignore the risks of standing up against apartheid or the possibility of personal harm. Instead, he weighed the potential impact and deemed his mission more significant than his fears. By breaking fear into manageable pieces, he reclaimed the mental and emotional space needed to act boldly.

Psychologists affirm that naming and examining fears reduces their emotional hold. When we quantify fear's likelihood and impact, we engage the logical part of our brain, reducing the grip of anxiety. This doesn't mean our fears vanish, but they become smaller and more manageable, allowing us to take steps forward.

As you create your Fear List, invite God into the process. Pray over each fear, asking Him to reveal His truth and provide His peace. Remember, God doesn't call us to face fear alone. His promise in Isaiah assures us that He strengthens and upholds us, even in the face of uncertainty.

By confronting your fears, you take away their power. Like Mandela, you can move forward with courage, knowing that fear is no longer an obstacle but an opportunity for growth and faith. With each fear you name and face, you'll find yourself walking in greater freedom, guided by God's steady hand.

> **"So do not fear, for I am with you; do not be dismayed, for I am your God. I will strengthen you and help you; I will uphold you with My righteous right hand."**
>
> — ISAIAH 41:10

LORD,

I bring my fears to You today. Help me to see them clearly,
to trust in Your power over them, and to find courage
through Your promises. Strengthen me, guide me,
and remind me that with You, I have nothing to fear.
Thank You for being my refuge and strength.

AMEN.

QUESTIONS TO CONSIDER:

1. What are the fears currently holding you back in your personal, professional, or spiritual life?
2. Are these fears based on real threats, or are they rooted in "what-ifs"?
3. How might these fears be impacting your decisions, relationships, or faith?
4. What has God said in His Word about fear, and how can you apply His promises to these situations?
5. What small, intentional step can you take today to move forward despite your fears?

RIGHT NOW:

- Create your Fear List. Write down all the fears weighing on your mind, no matter how big or small they seem.
- Next to each fear, rate its likelihood on a scale from 1 to 10. Then, rate its potential impact if it were to come true, also on a scale from 1 to 10.

THIS WEEK:

- Choose one fear from your list to address. Reflect on what actionable steps you can take to confront it, and commit to taking at least one small step forward.
- Pray over your Fear List daily, asking God for clarity, courage, and peace as you face each fear.
- Journal about how you feel after taking steps to confront one of your fears. What changed in your mindset or circumstances?

MOVING FORWARD:

- Repeat this process regularly to keep fear in check. Use your Fear List as a tool to name, evaluate, and confront new fears as they arise.
- Build a habit of replacing fear with faith by memorizing scripture like Isaiah 41:10 or Psalm 56:3: "When I am afraid, I put my trust in You."
- Share your progress with a trusted friend, mentor, or small group to celebrate victories and gain encouragement for ongoing growth.

Reminder:

Fear doesn't have the final say—God does. Trust in His strength, and take one bold step at a time.

Write "I Should" Thoughts

If you don't get out there and define yourself, you'll be quickly and inaccurately defined by others.

— MICHELLE OBAMA

I should have my life figured out by now." "I should be further along in my career." "I should be doing more to make everyone happy." Sound familiar? These "I should" thoughts creep in quietly, often disguised as helpful nudges, but they frequently stem from external expectations, misplaced guilt, or societal pressures that don't align with God's purpose for your life.

Michelle Obama, in her memoir *Becoming*, reflects on the trap of "shoulds." She shares, "If you don't get out there and define yourself, you'll be quickly and inaccurately defined by others." Her words highlight the importance of rejecting the narratives imposed by others and taking ownership of your identity. In another moment of clarity, she observes, "This may be the fundamental problem with caring a lot about what others think: It can put you on the established path—the my-isn't-that-impressive path—and keep you there for a long time." Obama's journey of questioning the expectations placed upon her is a testament to the transformative power of challenging the "I should" thoughts that weigh us down.

Romans 8:1 reminds us, "Therefore, there is now no condemnation for those who are in Christ Jesus." This verse serves as a powerful rebuttal to the guilt and shame often attached to our "shoulds." God doesn't measure our worth by societal standards or human expectations. His grace frees us from the burden of constantly trying to prove ourselves. Instead of being driven by "should," we are called to walk confidently in His purpose.

The problem with "I should" thoughts is that they often stem from fear, comparison, or people-pleasing rather than God's leading. They can create a false sense of inadequacy and distract us from what truly matters. Writing these thoughts down is the first step to breaking their hold. When you see them on paper, you can begin to question their source. Are they rooted in truth, or are they the result of societal expectations or internalized pressures?

Psychologists suggest reframing these thoughts as "I choose" statements. For example, instead of saying, "I should work harder to make everyone happy," you might write, "I choose to prioritize my well-being and trust that it's okay to say no." This shift empowers you to take responsibility for your decisions without being ruled by external pressures.

Michelle Obama's journey reminds us that authenticity comes from within. It's about aligning our actions with our values and not being swept along by the expectations of others. In the same way, Jesus' life was marked by purpose, not people-pleasing. He stayed true to His mission, even when it meant challenging cultural norms and facing criticism.

When you release the weight of "I should" and embrace God's grace, you'll find the freedom to walk confidently in His calling for your life. Let go of the guilt, and step boldly into the life He's prepared for you—not because you *should* but because you choose to follow His lead.

Therefore, there is now no condemnation for those who are in Christ Jesus.

— ROMANS 8:1

LORD,

I come to You with the weight of my "shoulds." Help me release the guilt, fear, and pressure that come with them. Teach me to discern between what You desire for me and what the world expects of me. Guide me to walk in the freedom of Your grace and purpose.

AMEN.

QUESTIONS TO CONSIDER:

1. What "I should" thoughts are most common in your life?
2. Where do these thoughts come from—societal expectations, personal fears, or comparison?
3. Do these "shoulds" align with God's truth and purpose for your life?
4. How might reframing these thoughts as "I choose" change the way you view your responsibilities?
5. How does Romans 8:1 encourage you to release the guilt tied to your "shoulds"?

RIGHT NOW:

- Write down your current "I should" thoughts. Be as specific as possible.
- Next to each thought, write where it comes from. Is it based on comparison, fear, guilt, or societal pressure?

THIS WEEK:

- Reframe each "I should" as an "I choose" statement. For example, "I should exercise more" becomes "I choose to make small, healthy decisions for my well-being." Reflect on how this reframe changes your mindset.
- Identify one "should" thought that has been weighing you down. Release it in prayer, asking God for guidance and peace to move forward.
- Spend ten minutes journaling about the difference between societal expectations and God's purpose for your life.

MOVING FORWARD:

- Make it a habit to question your "should" thoughts when they arise. Ask, "Is this something God is calling me to, or is it rooted in external pressures?"
- Practice replacing "I should" with "I choose" in your daily decisions.
- Share this process with a trusted friend or mentor, inviting them to hold you accountable and encourage you as you let go of unhealthy expectations.

Reminder:

In Christ, you are free to walk boldly in His purpose for your life, choosing grace over guilt and authenticity over approval.

Launch Your Legacy Project

The best way to find yourself is to lose yourself in the service of others.

— MAHATMA GANDHI

Jane Addams didn't set out to create history—she set out to help others. In 1889 she cofounded Hull House in Chicago, a settlement house aimed at serving the needs of the urban poor. From providing childcare and education to advocating for social reform, Hull House became a beacon of hope for countless immigrants and working-class families. But Addams's legacy didn't stop at meeting immediate needs. Her work laid the foundation for the modern social work profession and inspired movements that continue to shape public policy today.

Addams understood that true change wasn't just about addressing present issues but about building systems and structures that could endure beyond her lifetime. Her vision for Hull House was rooted in the belief that communities thrive when resources, education, and advocacy are accessible to all. Through her tireless efforts, Addams's legacy became one of service, compassion, and justice—a testament to the power of investing in something greater than oneself.

Matthew 5:16 reminds us, "Let your light shine before others, that they may see your good deeds and glorify your Father in heaven." A legacy project is an opportunity to let your light shine in a way that outlasts your own time on earth. It's about creating something that will continue to bless others, pointing them toward God's goodness long after you're gone.

The idea of a legacy project can feel daunting, but it doesn't have to be grand or complicated. Like Jane Addams, you can start by meeting a need right where you are. Perhaps it's mentoring a younger generation, creating a resource for your community, or advocating for a cause close to your heart. The key is to plant seeds that will grow, impacting lives in ways you may never fully see.

Research shows that people who engage in legacy-focused activities experience greater purpose and fulfillment. Studies from psychology and sociology confirm that contributing to something larger than oneself not only enhances well-being but also strengthens community bonds. Legacy work shifts the focus from individual achievement to collective impact, aligning beautifully with the biblical call to serve others.

Addams's example reminds us that legacy is not about personal recognition but about the lives touched through your efforts. She often worked behind the scenes, advocating for policies and reforms that would benefit generations to come. Her life demonstrates that a true legacy isn't measured in monuments but in the stories of those who were lifted up because of your faithfulness.

Jane Addams didn't know the full impact her work would have, but she trusted that sowing seeds of hope and justice would bear fruit. In the same way, you can trust that God will use your legacy project to glorify Him and bless others in ways beyond your imagination. Take the first step, let your light shine, and trust God to carry your work forward for His glory.

Let your light shine before others, that they may see your good deeds and glorify your Father in heaven.

— MATTHEW 5:16

LORD,

thank You for the gifts and opportunities You've given me to make a difference. Help me see the ways I can serve others and create something that glorifies You. Give me wisdom, courage, and perseverance as I take the first steps toward launching a legacy that reflects Your love and grace.

AMEN.

QUESTIONS TO CONSIDER:

1. What needs or issues in your community or circle of influence weigh heavily on your heart?
2. How has God uniquely equipped you—through your talents, experiences, or resources—to address these needs?
3. What small steps can you take today to begin laying the foundation for your legacy project?
4. How can you involve others to create a lasting impact beyond your individual efforts?
5. What fears or doubts are holding you back, and how can you trust God to guide you through them?

RIGHT NOW:

- Write down one area where you feel called to make a difference. Be specific about the need you want to address and how you feel God might be prompting you to act.
- Brainstorm three small, actionable steps you can take this week to begin working toward your legacy project.

THIS WEEK:

- Research existing organizations, resources, or mentors who can guide you or partner with you in launching your project.
- Reach out to one person who can help you refine your ideas or provide support.
- Pray over your vision, asking God to open doors, connect you with the right people, and show you the next steps.

MOVING FORWARD:

- Commit to setting aside a specific time each week to work on your legacy project.
- Begin documenting your progress, lessons learned, and the lives touched along the way. This will remind you of God's faithfulness and encourage you to keep going.
- Plan for sustainability. Think about how your project can continue to bless others even after you've stepped away. This might involve training others, creating resources, or forming partnerships.

Reminder:

Your legacy isn't about personal recognition but about the lives transformed through your obedience to God's call.

"To attain love,
peace, and joy,
turn your eyes
from the
temporal to
the eternal."

INTERVIEW 7:

Reclaiming Identity

BY: TERRY WRIGHT
PASTOR | RETIRED RADIO PRODUCER/HOST
DISCIPLE OF CHRIST | HUSBAND

1: What are you reigniting, reawakening, rediscovering, or reclaiming in this season?

A: At the tender age of eleven, I walked the aisle of my hometown church, a "girl-shy," self-conscious kid, choosing to pursue the narrow path of holiness. At nineteen, when friends introduced me to alcohol, I discovered a powerful ability to "communicate and persuade" others. That facade defined me for thirty-five years—until I lost it all and found Truth!

2: What challenges have you faced in this process, and what have they taught you?

A: I found completeness in my wife, Sally, who was seeking the Life in Christ I had abandoned. We began our pilgrimage for holiness together, but after seven years and financial success, I pulled her into my old ways. Then the most beautiful thing happened: We found riches in poverty, gain in loss, and joy in suffering!

As our world crumbled—creditors calling and old "friends" disappearing—our eyes turned back to Him. We realized He orchestrated both feast and famine to draw us back to His table. We've learned there is only one Bread and one Wine that satisfies. Indeed, the things that are seen are temporal, the unseen, eternal.

3: What unexpected joys or revelations have come from this process?

A: Recognizing that God desires to saturate us with His Being, empowering us to BE His offspring, we've tasted abundance hidden in lack. Loving the unlovely and blessing those who ignorantly hate us has proven to be "Christ-like." What joy!

4: Has this journey reshaped the way you define success or fulfillment? If so, how?

A: When we minister to the homeless, we share stories of our one-time wealth and how it "made itself wings," leaving me asking Sally if we have money for "handouts." Yet none can deny our claim to be the "Richest people they've ever met"—treasures safely deposited in the Bank of Heaven!

5: What advice would you give someone who feels stuck in a similar rut?

A: Jesus said, "Seek first the Kingdom of God, and these things will be added to you." Society overmarkets "things," but His promise of provision for earthly needs remains true. To attain love, peace, and joy, turn your eyes from the temporal to the eternal.

Create Mindset Metrics

Whether you think you can or you think you can't, you're right.

— HENRY FORD

Carol Dweck, a renowned psychologist and author, revolutionized the way we understand personal growth with her groundbreaking work on mindsets. Her research revealed the profound difference between a fixed mindset and a growth mindset. A fixed mindset clings to the belief that abilities and intelligence are static, often leading to fear of failure and avoidance of challenges. A growth mindset, on the other hand, embraces the idea that abilities can be developed through effort, learning, and persistence. Dweck's studies proved that shifting to a growth mindset can transform not only how we approach challenges but also how we perceive ourselves.

Romans 12:2 calls us to this same kind of transformation: "Do not conform to the pattern of this world, but be transformed by the renewing of your mind. Then you will be able to test and approve what God's will is—His good, pleasing and perfect will." Our thought patterns shape how we see the world, and God invites us to align our thinking with His truth. By renewing our minds, we free ourselves from limiting beliefs and open the door to the liberating power of His promises.

Creating "mindset metrics" is a practice inspired by Dweck's work and rooted in Scripture. It involves actively tracking the thoughts that limit or liberate you. Start by observing your inner dialogue. When you face a challenge, do you think, "I'll never figure this out" (fixed mindset), or “I can learn from this” (growth mindset)? When you make a mistake, do you dwell on failure, or do you reflect on the lessons it offers?

Recent research points to self-awareness as the first step toward meaningful change, verifying the power of monitoring and reframing thoughts. When we identify negative thought patterns, we can challenge them and replace them with truths that empower us. For example, instead of thinking, “I’m not good at this,” you might reframe it as, “I’m still learning, and that’s okay.” Over time, these shifts in perspective create a ripple effect, fostering resilience, creativity, and confidence.

Carol Dweck’s insights remind us that we have a choice in how we respond to our inner dialogue. Similarly, God’s Word equips us with the tools to confront lies and embrace His truth. Philippians 4:8 urges us to focus on what is true, noble, right, pure, lovely, admirable, excellent, and praiseworthy. When we align our thoughts with these qualities, we create space for the Holy Spirit to work within us, renewing our minds and transforming our lives.

As you begin tracking your mindset metrics, keep a journal to record moments when limiting thoughts arise. Write down the situation, the thought, and how you can reframe it in light of God’s truth. For example, a thought like “I’m not enough” can be countered with the reminder that you are fearfully and wonderfully made (Psalm 139:14).

Your mindset shapes your reality. By actively renewing your thoughts, you’re not only stepping into greater freedom but also becoming a vessel for God’s transformative power. Carol Dweck’s work and the wisdom of Scripture both affirm that growth is possible when we choose to align our minds with truth. As you track and transform your thoughts, you’ll find yourself walking in greater faith, purpose, and joy.

Do not conform to the pattern of this world, but be transformed by the renewing of your mind. Then you will be able to test and approve what God's will is—His good, pleasing and perfect will.

— ROMANS 12:2

LORD,
renew my mind so that my thoughts align with Your truth.
Help me recognize and replace limiting beliefs with
the confidence that comes from Your promises.
Guide me in embracing a growth mindset, so I can
approach challenges with courage and faith.
AMEN.

QUESTIONS TO CONSIDER:

1. What recurring negative thoughts or limiting beliefs have you been holding onto?
2. How do these thoughts affect the way you approach challenges or new opportunities?
3. In what areas of your life do you see evidence of a fixed mindset?
4. How can you actively reframe these thoughts into truths that align with God's Word?
5. How has God already equipped you to overcome the challenges you face?

RIGHT NOW:

- Write down three limiting thoughts you've had. For each, identify the fixed mindset belief and reframe it as a growth mindset statement. Example: Limiting Thought: "I'll never get this right." Reframed Thought: "I can learn and improve with God's help."

THIS WEEK:

- Begin a Mindset Metrics Journal. Each day, note one moment when a limiting belief surfaced. Write down the thought, the context, and how you reframed it.
- Memorize Philippians 4:8 and use it to shift your focus to what is true, noble, and praiseworthy.
- Choose one area of your life (work, relationships, spiritual growth) where you'd like to embrace a growth mindset, and commit to taking one small action in that area.

MOVING FORWARD:

- Regularly review your Mindset Metrics Journal to identify patterns.
- Practice gratitude by listing three things you learned or overcame each week.
- Incorporate prayer into your thought-monitoring process, inviting God to transform your perspective daily.

Reminder:

By aligning your mindset with God's truth, you unlock the freedom, growth, and transformation He has planned for you.

Phone a Friend

Where you go, I will go, and where you lodge, I will lodge; your people shall be my people, and your God my God.

— RUTH

Sometimes the people closest to us see things we can't see in ourselves. In moments of uncertainty or self-doubt, their words can remind us of strengths we've overlooked and gifts we've taken for granted. This is beautifully illustrated in the story of Ruth and Naomi in the Bible.

When Naomi's life seemed to crumble—after losing her husband and sons—she decided to return to Bethlehem, urging her daughters-in-law to go back to their own families. Ruth, however, refused to leave Naomi's side. In Ruth 1:16, she famously declares, "Where you go, I will go, and where you stay, I will stay. Your people will be my people and your God my God." Ruth's unwavering loyalty and determination weren't just acts of kindness; they were reflections of her incredible strength and character.

Naomi, in turn, recognized Ruth's resilience and resourcefulness. She encouraged Ruth to glean in the fields of Boaz, subtly guiding her toward opportunities that would eventually lead to security and restoration. Their relationship was marked by mutual encouragement, with each woman speaking life into the other when it was most needed. Naomi helped Ruth see her worth and potential, while Ruth's steadfastness gave Naomi hope.

This dynamic of mutual affirmation underscores the power of close relationships. First Thessalonians 5:11 reminds us to "encourage one another and build each other up," showing that God often uses the people around us to reveal our strengths and callings. Seeking feedback from trusted friends or family can be a transformative practice, one that brings clarity and confidence in seasons of doubt.

Modern psychology also affirms the value of feedback from trusted voices, saying that feedback from close relationships can boost self-awareness and self-esteem, helping us identify strengths we might otherwise dismiss or overlook. By listening to the affirmations of those who know us well, we can gain insights into how our unique gifts bless others and glorify God.

When you ask those closest to you to name your strengths, you're inviting them to reflect back the light they see in you—a light you might not fully recognize on your own.

As you begin this process, approach it with humility and openness. Choose three people who know you well and who you trust to be honest and supportive. Ask them questions like, "What do you think I'm naturally good at?" or "How do you see me making a difference in the lives of others?" Their answers may surprise you, offering affirmations that uplift your spirit and challenge you to live out your strengths with greater purpose.

The story of Ruth and Naomi reminds us that we don't journey through life alone. God places people in our lives to encourage and build us up, reflecting His love and purpose. When we invite their voices into our reflections, we not only gain clarity about our strengths but also deepen the bonds of trust and love that sustain us.

Encourage one another and build each other up, just as in fact you are doing.

— I THESSALONIANS 5:11

LORD,

thank You for the gift of relationships and
the people You've placed in my life to encourage me.
Help me to approach them with humility,
to listen with an open heart, and to see myself
through their eyes as You see me.

AMEN.

QUESTIONS TO CONSIDER:

1. Who are the people in your life you trust to speak truth and encouragement into your journey?
2. What qualities or strengths do you hope they might recognize in you?
3. How can you invite these trusted voices to help you identify and affirm your God-given gifts?
4. In what ways can you offer encouragement and affirmation to others in return?
5. How might these conversations deepen your relationships and strengthen your faith?

RIGHT NOW:

- Identify three trusted people who know you well and can offer honest, affirming feedback.
- Reach out to them with intentional questions like, "What do you think I'm naturally gifted at?" or "How do you see me making a difference?"

THIS WEEK:

- Reflect on the insights and affirmations you receive. Journal how their words impact your perspective on your strengths and calling.
- Look for opportunities to offer encouragement and affirmation to others in your circle.

MOVING FORWARD:

- Make it a habit to regularly check in with your trusted circle for feedback and support.
- Keep a record of affirmations you receive and revisit them when you face self-doubt.
- Continue to build others up, creating a cycle of mutual encouragement that reflects God's love.

Reminder:

God uses relationships to reveal your gifts and strengthen your purpose. Trust the voices He's placed in your life, and let them remind you of the unique light you bring to the world.

Do Value Verification

Our values should be so crystalized in our minds
that they don't feel like a choice.
— BRENE BROWN

Values are like a compass, pointing us in the direction we say we want to go. But having a compass isn't enough—we need a map to ensure we're on the right path. The compass shows us our destination, but the map reveals whether our steps are truly aligned with the course we've set. In the same way, it's one thing to say we value kindness, faith, or discipline; it's another to let our daily actions reflect those values.

James 1:22 reminds us, "Do not merely listen to the word, and so deceive yourselves. Do what it says." This verse challenges us to move beyond professing our beliefs to living them out. It's easy to claim a value system that sounds noble, but our true character is revealed in the choices we make, especially when no one is watching.

Consider the analogy of a hiker on a journey. The hiker's compass is calibrated to always point north, symbolizing their values. However, the hiker must still consult the map to ensure they are following the correct path. Without consistent checks, even the most well-meaning hiker can stray off course. Similarly, in our daily lives, it's important to regularly evaluate whether our actions align with the values we claim to hold dear.

Studies in psychology affirm the importance of congruence between values and actions. Data confirms that individuals who align their behaviors with their core values experience greater life satisfaction, reduced stress, and a stronger sense of purpose. When our actions are inconsistent with our values, we experience cognitive dissonance—a mental discomfort that arises when our behavior doesn't match our beliefs. This tension can serve as a powerful motivator to reassess and realign.

Think about your own life. What do you say you value? Perhaps it's family, faith, honesty, or generosity. Now consider: Do your daily choices reflect these values? If you claim to value family, are you making time for meaningful connections? If faith is a priority, are you spending time in prayer or Scripture? If you value generosity, are you actively giving your time, resources, or encouragement to others?

The apostle Paul's writings often emphasize the importance of living out our faith. He reminds us that our actions serve as a testimony to what we truly believe. Aligning our actions with our values not only strengthens our relationship with God but also serves as a light to others, inspiring them to live with integrity.

Living in alignment with your values doesn't mean perfection—it means intentionality. Just as a hiker occasionally pauses to check their map and compass, we must regularly assess whether our actions reflect the life we want to lead. Take time to reflect on your priorities, and invite God into the process. He is faithful to guide and correct us when we veer off course.

When we practice value verification, we live with greater clarity and purpose. Our lives become a reflection of what we hold most dear, and in doing so, we honor the One who called us to walk in truth and love.

Do not merely listen to the word, and so deceive yourselves. Do what it says.

— JAMES 1:22

LORD,
help me to live with integrity and courage, aligning my actions with the values You have placed on my heart. Guide me to walk in truth and love so that my life reflects Your purpose and grace.
AMEN.

QUESTIONS TO CONSIDER:

1. What are the core values you claim to live by, and why are they important to you?
2. In what areas of your life do your actions align with your values, and where do they fall short?
3. What small adjustments can you make to bring your behavior more in line with your beliefs?
4. How do your values reflect your faith and calling as a follower of Christ?
5. Who or what can help hold you accountable to live out your values daily?

RIGHT NOW:

- Write a list of your top five values and reflect on how they influence your decisions and actions.
- Evaluate whether your current routines, habits, and relationships align with these values.

THIS WEEK:

- Choose one value to focus on and identify a specific way to practice it more intentionally in your daily life.
- Reflect on the connection between your faith and your values, asking God to reveal areas for growth.

MOVING FORWARD:

- Make it a habit to review your values monthly, considering how well your life reflects them.
- Share your values and progress with a trusted friend, mentor, or small group for encouragement and accountability.
- Commit to practicing value verification regularly as a spiritual and personal discipline.

Reminder:

Your values are a reflection of your faith and purpose. Aligning your actions with them helps you live with clarity, integrity, and deeper connection to God's plan for your life.

Circle Back to Childhood

It is never too late to be what you might have been.

— GEORGE ELIOT

As a child, Beatrix Potter spent her days sketching the animals she observed in her countryside home. Her fascination with nature and her talent for illustration were clear from an early age. But like many of us, life moved her away from those childhood pursuits. She grew up, faced family expectations, and found herself navigating a world that didn't always nurture creativity.

Years later, at age thirty-six, Beatrix decided to revisit those early hobbies. She began illustrating and writing again, drawing on the memories and passions of her youth. What started as a letter to cheer up a friend's child became the basis for her beloved book, *The Tale of Peter Rabbit*. Reconnecting with her childhood interests didn't just bring her joy—it launched her into a career that has inspired generations of readers and artists. Beatrix's story is a beautiful reminder that the things we loved as children often hold clues to the purpose and creativity God placed in us.

Matthew 18:3 (ESV) says, "Truly, I say to you, unless you turn and become like children, you will never enter the kingdom of heaven." While this verse speaks to childlike faith, it also reminds us of the importance of childlike wonder. Children find joy in simplicity. They create, explore, and dream without fear of judgment or failure. Reconnecting with the hobbies of your childhood is a way to tap into that wonder, allowing God to renew your spirit and reignite your sense of purpose.

What did you love to do as a child? Maybe you loved painting, writing stories, dancing, or building things with your hands. Perhaps you had a fascination with nature, music, or tinkering with machines. Those hobbies weren't just activities; they were ways God uniquely wired you to express creativity and joy. When we revisit these passions as adults, we often find that they still hold a special place in our hearts—and they can even be a source of healing, inspiration, or connection to God.

Research shows that engaging in hobbies you enjoy can reduce stress, boost creativity, and improve overall well-being. But beyond the science, there's a deeper truth: These activities allow us to reflect God's nature as the ultimate Creator. When you draw, write, bake, or garden, you're not just engaging in a pastime—you're participating in an act of worship, using the gifts God gave you to bring joy to yourself and others.

I hope Beatrix Potter's story reminds you that it's never too late to reconnect with the things that once brought you joy. Whether you revisit an old passion for the sake of creativity, relaxation, or simply for fun, it's an opportunity to see how God can use even the smallest of hobbies to bring growth and renewal.

Today, take a moment to think about the hobbies you loved as a child. What's stopping you from picking them up again? It's never too late to rediscover the joy, wonder, and creativity God has placed in you.

> **Truly, I say to you, unless you turn and become like children, you will never enter the kingdom of heaven.**
>
> — MATTHEW 18:3 (ESV)

LORD,
thank You for the gifts and passions You placed in me, even from childhood. Help me to reconnect with the wonder and joy of those early interests. Use them to renew my spirit and draw me closer to You.
AMEN.

QUESTIONS TO CONSIDER:

1. What hobbies or activities brought you joy as a child?
2. Why did you stop engaging in those activities, and how might they fit into your life now?
3. How can revisiting these passions help you reconnect with the creativity and wonder God placed in you?
4. What small step can you take this week to reintroduce a childhood hobby into your routine?
5. How can these activities bring you closer to God or serve as an act of worship?

RIGHT NOW:

- Write a list of your favorite childhood hobbies or activities. Reflect on how they made you feel and why they were important to you.
- Identify one activity you'd like to revisit, and gather the materials or tools you'll need to start.

THIS WEEK:

- Set aside thirty minutes to engage in your chosen childhood hobby. Approach it with curiosity and joy, letting go of perfection or expectations.
- Reflect in a journal about how it felt to reconnect with this activity. Did it spark creativity, joy, or a sense of peace?

MOVING FORWARD:

- Make time weekly or monthly to continue exploring this or other childhood hobbies.
- Look for ways to incorporate these activities into your spiritual practices, such as journaling prayers while drawing or reflecting on God's creation while gardening.
- Share your experiences with a trusted friend or mentor, inviting them to explore their own childhood joys alongside you.

Reminder:

It's never too late to rediscover the joy God planted in you as a child. Reconnecting with your passions can renew your spirit and remind you of His creativity and love.

Create Your Daily Minimum

You do not rise to the level of your goals.

You fall to the level of your systems.

— JAMES CLEAR

In the sixth century, St. Benedict of Nursia created a guide for monastic life known as the Rule of St. Benedict. This rule provided a structured rhythm of daily practices, including prayer, work, and study, that grounded the lives of monks in discipline and purpose. It wasn't about grand gestures or unattainable goals; it was about small, consistent actions that built a life of devotion, community, and spiritual growth. The Rule emphasized the importance of creating sustainable habits—what we might now call nonnegotiable daily practices—to cultivate a meaningful and balanced life.

Centuries later, James Clear's *Atomic Habits* reinforces this same principle. Clear writes that small, consistent habits can lead to profound transformation over time. Rather than focusing on lofty goals, Clear encourages readers to focus on the systems and routines that will lead to those outcomes. He emphasizes the importance of establishing "minimum habits," or small, manageable actions that build momentum and consistency.

Joshua 1:8 underscores this idea in a spiritual context: "Keep this Book of the Law always on your lips; meditate on it day and night, so that you may be careful to do everything written in it. Then you will be prosperous and successful." Success and spiritual growth are not the result of occasional effort but of consistent faithfulness in the small things.

Imagine your day as a foundation. What are the nonnegotiable practices that will ensure it's solid and steady? These might include prayer, a moment of gratitude, a few minutes of reading Scripture, or even something as simple as drinking a glass of water to start your morning. Like the Rule of St. Benedict or Clear's concept of atomic habits, these small actions are the building blocks of a life aligned with your values and God's purpose.

Research supports this approach. Studies in behavioral psychology express that small, consistent actions are far more effective than sporadic, ambitious efforts. These habits create neural pathways in the brain that make behaviors automatic over time. When you establish a "daily minimum," you're not just completing tasks—you're training your mind and spirit to live intentionally.

Both St. Benedict's Rule and James Clear's insights remind us that we don't have to overhaul our entire lives to experience growth. Instead, we can focus on a few key practices that anchor our days and shape our character.

As you establish your daily minimum, remember that God is with you in the process. He doesn't expect perfection, but He delights in your faithfulness. Like a steady stream carving a path through rock, your daily practices have the power to shape your heart, mind, and spirit in profound ways. With each step, you're not only building a routine—you're building a life grounded in His grace and purpose.

Keep this Book of the Law always on your lips; meditate on it day and night, so that you may be careful to do everything written in it. Then you will be prosperous and successful.

— JOSHUA 1:8

LORD,

help me to focus on small, faithful steps each day. Teach me to build habits that honor You and align my heart with Your purpose. Thank You for guiding me in both the big and small things.

AMEN.

QUESTIONS TO CONSIDER:

1. What small, consistent habits would help you live in alignment with your faith and values?
2. Are there current practices you can build on to create momentum in your daily life?
3. What is one nonnegotiable practice you can commit to, no matter how busy the day becomes?
4. How can you ensure your daily minimum includes time with God?
5. How might small, faithful actions transform your long-term spiritual and personal growth?

RIGHT NOW:

- Write down three small, achievable habits you can incorporate into your day as your "daily minimum." Keep them simple and realistic, such as five minutes of prayer, a single verse of Scripture, or journaling one gratitude note.

THIS WEEK:

- Practice your daily minimum every day, keeping track of your consistency. Focus on progress, not perfection.
- Reflect in your journal at the end of the week: How did these small habits shape your mindset, energy, or connection with God?

MOVING FORWARD:

- Gradually build on your daily minimum. Once your habits feel automatic, consider adding or extending them (e.g., moving from five minutes of prayer to ten).
- Share your daily minimum with a friend or mentor to build accountability and encouragement.
- Revisit your habits monthly to ensure they continue to align with your values and goals.

Reminder:

Transformation starts with faithfulness in the small things. Build habits that anchor your day in God's purpose, and trust Him to guide your growth.

Write a Perfect Day

Success is peace of mind, which is a direct result of self-satisfaction in knowing you did your best to become the best that you are capable of becoming.

— JOHN WOODEN

John Wooden, famously known as the "Wiz of Westwood," is celebrated as one of the greatest basketball coaches in history. During his tenure at UCLA, he led his team to ten NCAA national championships in twelve years. While his record-breaking accomplishments are legendary, Wooden's true legacy lies in his philosophy of intentional living and daily preparation.

Wooden didn't believe success was defined by winning games or accumulating accolades. Instead, he saw it as the culmination of deliberate effort and purposeful living. Every day, Wooden planned his hours meticulously, ensuring that his actions reflected his values. He emphasized the importance of preparation, famously saying, "Failing to prepare is preparing to fail." Wooden's structured approach to his days allowed him to build a life of meaning and impact, both on and off the court.

Proverbs 16:9 reminds us, "In their hearts humans plan their course, but the LORD establishes their steps." This verse beautifully illustrates the balance between human intention and divine guidance. God calls us to steward our time wisely, but we must also leave room for His direction. Writing a "perfect day" isn't about creating a rigid schedule but about envisioning a life that aligns with God's purpose for you.

The practice of crafting your ideal day can be transformative. When you imagine your perfect day hour by hour, you gain clarity about what truly matters to you. Are you prioritizing meaningful work, quality time with loved ones, or moments of worship and reflection? Writing it down helps you identify the values you want to live by and the habits that support them.

Research in psychology highlights the power of visualization in achieving goals. Athletes, like Wooden's players, often use mental imagery to improve performance. Similarly, envisioning your ideal day creates a mental blueprint that motivates you to take intentional steps toward that vision.

Wooden's daily routine included moments of reflection, preparation, and gratitude. He believed that success was not measured by external achievements but by the peace that comes from knowing you gave your best effort. His approach serves as a reminder that a "perfect day" isn't about perfection but about living in alignment with your values.

Take a moment to consider what your perfect day might look like. How would you start your morning? What activities would fill your hours? Who would you spend time with? At the end of the day, what would leave you feeling fulfilled and grateful? As you write it down, invite God into the process. Ask Him to reveal His plans for you and to guide your steps.

Let your perfect day be a reflection of your faith, your values, and your desire to make the most of the time you've been given. And remember, the ultimate measure of a perfect day isn't how much you accomplish but how closely you walk with God in the process.

In their hearts humans plan their course, but the LORD establishes their steps.

— PROVERBS 16:9

LORD,
thank You for the gift of today. Help me to align my plans with Your purpose and guide my steps as I strive to live intentionally. May my days reflect Your will and bring glory to Your name.
AMEN.

QUESTIONS TO CONSIDER:

1. What would a day aligned with your values, faith, and purpose look like?
2. How would you structure your morning to set the tone for the rest of the day?
3. What activities bring you joy, fulfillment, and connection with God and others?
4. How would you balance productivity, rest, and relationships throughout the day?
5. What practices would help you end your day with gratitude and peace?

RIGHT NOW:

- Write out your "perfect day" from morning to night. Be specific about what activities, people, and priorities would make it meaningful.
- Identify three key habits or practices that you can begin incorporating into your real daily routine to move closer to your vision.

THIS WEEK:

- Implement one part of your "perfect day" into your current routine. It could be a morning prayer, an afternoon walk, or a dedicated time for reflection.
- Journal each evening about how it felt to align a part of your day with your ideal vision. Did it bring you closer to peace, joy, or purpose?

MOVING FORWARD:

- Use your "perfect day" as a guiding framework, adjusting it as needed to reflect God's leading in your life.
- Regularly revisit and refine your daily routine to ensure it aligns with your values and priorities.
- Share your perfect day vision with a trusted friend or mentor and invite them to hold you accountable to your intentions.

Reminder:

A perfect day isn't about perfection—it's about living intentionally, with God at the center, one faithful step at a time.

Create "Life Categories"

The key is in not spending time, but in investing it.

— STEPHEN COVEY

Stephen Covey, the renowned author of *The 7 Habits of Highly Effective People*, dedicated his life to helping others achieve balance and purpose. He believed that true effectiveness comes from investing in all areas of life—not just work or personal achievement but in relationships, health, and spiritual growth as well. Covey often spoke about the importance of aligning daily actions with long-term values and emphasized living a life of harmony across all areas.

One of Covey's most impactful teachings was his emphasis on balance. He encouraged people to evaluate their lives holistically, breaking life into key categories like physical health, emotional well-being, relationships, career, spirituality, and recreation. This approach mirrors the concept of the "Wheel of Life," a tool often used to assess satisfaction in different areas. If one section of the wheel is neglected, it creates imbalance, making the "ride" of life bumpy and unsustainable.

Luke 2:52 provides a biblical framework for balanced living: "Jesus grew in wisdom and stature, and in favor with God and man." This verse highlights Jesus' development in four key areas: intellectual ("wisdom"), physical ("stature"), spiritual ("favor with God"), and social ("favor with man"). Just as Jesus modeled a life of balance and growth, we, too, are called to steward our lives holistically, tending to each area with intentionality.

Creating life categories allows us to assess where we are thriving and where we might need growth. Consider the areas Covey and the Wheel of Life suggest: relationships, health, career, finances, spirituality, recreation, personal growth, and contribution. Rate your satisfaction in each category on a scale from 1 to 10. Are there areas where you're flourishing? Are there areas where you've been running on empty?

Positive psychologists declare that living a balanced life contributes to overall well-being and resilience. Studies from positive psychology reveal that neglecting one area of life often leads to stress and dissatisfaction in others. For example, overworking at the expense of relationships can result in loneliness, while neglecting health can reduce energy and productivity in other areas.

Covey's teachings align wonderfully with this principle. He stressed that small, consistent investments in all areas of life lead to lasting success and fulfillment. This doesn't mean every area will be perfectly balanced at all times, but it does mean prioritizing intentionality and alignment with your values.

As you reflect on your own "life categories," invite God into the process. Ask Him to reveal areas where you need growth and strength to make changes. Perhaps your spiritual life needs more attention, or maybe it's time to invest in relationships that have been neglected. Remember, living a balanced life is not about perfection; it's about faithfulness and stewardship.

Stephen Covey's legacy reminds us that balance is a choice. As you create and evaluate your life categories, let them serve as a tool to guide you closer to the life God has called you to live.

Jesus grew in wisdom and stature, and in favor with God and man.

—LUKE 2:52

LORD,

help me steward my life with balance and intentionality. Show me where I need to grow, and guide me as I align every area of my life with Your purpose.

AMEN.

QUESTIONS TO CONSIDER:

1. What are the most important areas of your life that need consistent attention and care?
2. How do your current habits and priorities align with your values in each category?
3. Are there any areas where you feel unfulfilled or overextended?
4. What small steps can you take to invest in the areas you've been neglecting?
5. How can you invite God into each category of your life to experience growth and balance?

RIGHT NOW:

- List your life categories (e.g., health, relationships, career, finances, spirituality, recreation, personal growth, contribution).
- Rate your satisfaction in each category on a scale from 1 to 10. Reflect on areas that are thriving and areas that need more attention.

THIS WEEK:

- Choose one category to focus on improving. Set a specific, achievable goal for that area (e.g., scheduling a family dinner, taking a daily walk, or dedicating ten minutes to prayer).
- Track your efforts and reflect on how they impact your overall sense of balance and fulfillment.

MOVING FORWARD:

- Revisit your life categories regularly (e.g., monthly or quarterly) to reassess and adjust your goals.
- Build habits that support holistic growth in all areas of your life, even in small ways.
- Share your categories and goals with a trusted friend or mentor for encouragement and accountability.

Reminder:

Balance is not about perfection but about intentional stewardship. Small, consistent steps across all areas of life lead to lasting peace and purpose.

Write Your Mission

What we see and celebrate in the world begins with what we value in ourselves.

— UNKNOWN

Fred Rogers, lovingly known as Mr. Rogers, built his entire life and career on a singular, unwavering mission: to create a space where children could feel seen, loved, and valued. From his quiet demeanor to his thoughtful words, every part of his work reflected his purpose. In a world filled with noise and distraction, Rogers provided a sanctuary of gentleness and care. His mission wasn't about fame or recognition but about showing kindness and compassion in the simplest, most profound ways.

Rogers's ability to focus on his mission allowed him to craft a legacy that continues to shape the future. He once said, "We live in a world in which we need to share responsibility. It's easy to say, 'It's not my child, not my community, not my world, not my problem.' Then there are those who see the need and respond. I consider those people my heroes." This statement encapsulates his mission—a commitment to making the world a kinder, more understanding place by meeting people where they are.

Ephesians 2:10 reminds us, "We are God's handiwork, created in Christ Jesus to do good works, which God prepared in advance for us to do." Each of us has a unique purpose, a calling that only we can fulfill. Crafting your personal mission is an exercise in aligning with God's plan for your life. It's about distilling your values, passions, and gifts into a clear statement that can guide your choices and actions.

Fred Rogers's example shows us that a mission doesn't have to be grandiose or complicated. In fact, the most impactful missions are often the simplest. Rogers's focus on kindness, understanding, and connection changed lives because he lived his mission daily. Whether it was tying his sneakers or singing a song, every action reflected his purpose.

Psychologists note that having a clear sense of purpose increases resilience, motivation, and overall well-being. When we know our mission, we're better equipped to navigate challenges and stay grounded in what truly matters. Spiritually, crafting a mission helps us stay focused on the work God has set before us, reminding us that our lives are part of a greater story.

Take a moment to reflect on your own mission. What values drive you? What gifts has God given you to share with the world? Your mission might be about fostering creativity, advocating for justice, or nurturing relationships. Whatever it is, keep it simple and authentic. Aim for fifteen words or less—a concise statement that can serve as a compass for your life.

Fred Rogers didn't try to be everything to everyone. He focused on his unique calling, trusting that his faithfulness to his mission would bear fruit. And it did. As you write your personal mission, remember that God has already equipped you for the work He's called you to do. Embrace it, live it, and let your mission be a light that shines in the lives of others.

We are God's handiwork, created in Christ Jesus to do good works, which God prepared in advance for us to do.

— EPHESIANS 2:10

LORD,

help me to discover and embrace the purpose You've placed in my life. Guide me as I align my values, gifts, and actions with Your plan, and use my mission to reflect Your love and grace to others.

AMEN.

QUESTIONS TO CONSIDER:

1. What values are most important to you, and how do they shape your daily decisions?
2. What unique gifts or passions has God given you to share with the world?
3. Who or what do you feel called to serve or impact through your life's work?
4. How can you align your actions and goals with God's greater purpose for your life?
5. If your life's mission were summed up in one sentence, what would it say?

RIGHT NOW:

- Reflect on your values, passions, and gifts. Write down key words or phrases that describe what drives you and what you feel called to do.
- Draft a mission statement in fifteen words or less. Keep it concise and authentic, reflecting what matters most to you.

THIS WEEK:

- Post your mission statement somewhere visible (e.g., a journal, mirror, or phone wallpaper) as a daily reminder.
- Look for one way each day to live out your mission, whether in small acts or larger decisions.
- Share your mission statement with a trusted friend or mentor for feedback and encouragement.

MOVING FORWARD:

- Revisit your mission statement periodically to refine or adjust it as God's calling becomes clearer.
- Use your mission as a guide for setting goals, making decisions, and evaluating how you spend your time.
- Reflect on how your mission impacts others and aligns with God's greater plan for your life.

Reminder:

Your mission is not about perfection but faithfulness. Live it daily, trusting God to use your efforts for His glory.

Dear Friend,

This book was prayerfully crafted with you, the reader, in mind. Every word, every sentence, every page was thoughtfully written, designed, and packaged to encourage you—right where you are this very moment. At DaySpring, our vision is to see every person experience the life-changing message of God's love. So, as we worked through rough drafts, design changes, edits, and details, we prayed for you to deeply experience His unfailing love, indescribable peace, and pure joy. It is our sincere hope that through these Truth-filled pages your heart will be blessed, knowing that God cares about you—your desires and disappointments, your challenges and dreams.

He knows. He cares. He loves you unconditionally.

BLESSINGS!
THE DAYSPRING BOOK TEAM